PRAISE FOR *A NEW THEORY OF TEENAGERS*

"Remarkably intelligent. . . . No doubt will this help parents understand not only what is at stake, but how they can make the highest and greatest purpose of their role as parents."

—Michael B. Finkelstein, MD, FACP, ABIHM

"Inspirational and enlightening . . . new ways of looking at age-old interpersonal challenges with teens and important others in our lives."

—Thomas Monaco, Executive Director, Experienced Professionals Career Management, Columbia Business School, Career Management Center

"Dr. Santangelo wisely guides parents and others who work with teens in developing their own strengths for this challenging time. *A New Theory of Teenagers* is both an innovative and supportive guide for this journey."

—Lynn Ponton, MD, author of *The Romance of Risk* and *The Sex Lives of Teenagers*

"A nuanced and compelling explanation of how parental and adolescent issues sometimes clash to produce superficially inexplicable behavioral problems in the adolescent. [Dr. Santangelo's] solution: a therapy model in which both parents and adolescents learn about themselves so that they can change the toxic interactions in which they are engaged. Movement almost always requires change—self-recognition and growth—for parent and adolescent, with the result being a richer, fuller, and more harmonious inner and outer existence for everyone."

—Glen Elliott, Chief Psychiatrist and Medical Director, Children's Health Council

"Dr. Christa Santangelo, expertly weaves her vast experience working with adolescence and their parents, her knowledge of research, and understanding of human emotions, thoughts, and behaviors to present us with this profound, easy to read and enjoyable book on how best to deal the turbulent teenage years. But this is far more than a read for parents of teens. It is for anyone trying to understand themselves, their feelings and actions, and learn tools to better navigate their lives to be more satisfying and fulfilling. Dr. Santangelo provides us with a host of practical mind-body techniques that are tremendously beneficial to deepen our connection with ourselves and others and no doubt, improve our relationships with our children. Dr. Santangelo's use of case examples is riveting and educational and greatly enriches the messages in this book. This is a must read for all parents! Praise for *A New Theory of Teenagers*."

—RHONDA S. ADESSKY, PhD, Clinical Director, the Training Center for Mind Body Skills, and author, *Mind Body Fertility Manual (Unpublished Manuscript)*

"*A New Theory of Teenagers* is bound to be a must-read for parents . . . Its wise counseling and real-life practical examples reminded me of another parenting must-read: *What to Expect When You're Expecting*. Dr. Christa Santangelo is that earthy, insightful health professional we all seek when we've run out of answers and are not even sure what questions to be asking."   —TOM ALLON, President/CEO, City & State

"Dr. Santangelo's work *A New Theory of Teenagers* defines a positive approach to watershed moments for struggling parents of teens. She motivates parents to positively support their teens' 'birth' to adulthood through actualization of their own best selves. She argues that parenting a teen necessarily reawakens that parent's own journey to adulthood. Parents need to work with their identification with the emotionality of teen experience—and becoming mindful of whether requirements for teen conduct might be a reflection of their own over-idealizations. Using love to give permission to create space for more mindful parent-teen transactions forms the basis for Dr. Santangelo's clear and powerful therapeutic approach."

—BRYNA SIEGEL, PhD, Founder and Executive Director, Autism Center of Northern California, Professor, Child & Adolescent Psychiatry, University of California, San Francisco (retired)

A NEW THEORY OF TEENAGERS

Seven Transformational Strategies
to Empower You and Your Teen

Christa Santangelo, PhD

SEAL PRESS

Seal Press
Hachette Book Group
1290 Avenue of the Americas, New York, NY 10104
www.sealpress.com
@sealpress

Printed in the United States of America
First Edition: November 2018

Published by Seal Press, an imprint of Perseus Books, LLC, a subsidiary of Hachette Book Group, Inc. The Seal Press name and logo is a trademark of the Hachette Book Group.

The publisher is not responsible for websites (or their content) that are not owned by the publisher.

All of the individuals discussed reflect composites designed to illustrate a variety of experiences, problems, and solutions. No real names are used, and identifying details have been changed.

Print book interior design by Linda Mark

Library of Congress Cataloging-in-Publication Data has been applied for.
ISBNs: 978-1-58005-832-2 (paperback), 978-1-58005-831-5 (ebook)

LSC-C

10 9 8 7 6 5 4 3 2 1

For Natasha

CONTENTS

INTRODUCTION

There is no greater agony than bearing an untold story inside you.

—Zora Neale Hurston

I WROTE THIS BOOK. OR DID THIS BOOK WRITE ME? AS a psychologist trained at Yale, and an assistant clinical professor at the University of California, San Francisco, I specialize in adolescents and their families. In addition to studying traditional methods of psychology (psycho-analytic attachment, cognitive and dialectical behavioral therapy, and others), I have also trained in mind-body medicine: yoga, meditation, and energy healing. After two decades of listening to tales of love lost and love found between parents and their adolescents, I thought I knew something about the parent/child relationship.

So where were all those brilliant philosophies and practices when I got a text from my daughter's babysitter after a long day with patients? "Your daughter is in the ER. Come quickly." Heart racing, body in fight-or-flight mode, I flew the few blocks to the local emergency room to find my darling daughter hooked up to every imaginable machine and tube. "Mamaaaaaaaaah," she wailed as she caught sight of me through the maze of wires and beeping monitors. My mind was racing, and any emotional clarity I had was held together only by sheer necessity and faith. Immediately, I questioned myself. Was it my fault? Why did I have to be a working mom? Bad choice. Idiot. Would she be okay? How much trauma had she endured?

The specter of losing a child may be one of the most primitive fears a parent can face. In small doses it motivates us to be the best parents we can be. In large doses it threatens the delicate relationship we are forging with this developing human in our midst: bringing our own trauma to our child is too heavy a burden for their small psyches to bear. Thankfully, my daughter fully healed after this rope-swing adventure gone awry, with the help of an angelic team of competent doctors. She was fine. I wasn't!

I wrote this book as much for me as for you. What I have found over the course of treating hundreds of teens and parents is that our teens are our mirrors for our deepest selves. They reflect our fears, our love, and any other emotion we are embodying or projecting. The challenges our teens face are often reflections of our own unresolved dilemmas, whether mild or severe: repressed hurt, unacknowledged insecurities, unspoken anxieties. All of these things we so skillfully bury suddenly become unearthed by the presence of a teen. But by looking inward and employing certain strategies we can empower our teens *and* ourselves.

Parenting a teen is a particular type of two-dimensional birth. And just like birth, it involves magnificent pain and equally magnificent pleasure. It is also a teen's job to birth herself and to continue to love herself through the process. As a parent, you may encounter aspects of your budding adult that you find unlovable, whether you wish to admit it or not, and the birth can become complicated. Power struggles, despairing parents, and alienated teens are some of the manifestations of this stifled process. Of course there are moments for appropriate reactions to their annoying, egregious, rude, and otherwise objectionable behaviors. And some teens come by their challenges through their own biology, character, or other means, which have nothing to do with the parent. But I have found these cases to be rare.

My observations have led me to the belief that if parents fail to look within to see where their fears or issues may be complicating the process of their teen giving birth to himself, not only might their teen's evolution into adulthood become stifled, but they will also have missed an opportunity for transformation in their own life. The challenge is that our fears are often unconscious, so it takes some time and strategic intervention to find them and bring them forward so they do not interfere with our relationships. Ultimately, your teen's problems—substance abuse, depression, eating disorders, anxiety, and even less serious ones like poor communication and existential confusion—are like rich soil for both your child and yourself.

Parenting is a journey with potential for unimaginable rewards. Your teen is learning through experimentation, which often leads to uncomfortable outcomes, from disappointment with friends to terrifying visits to the emergency room. However, with the right, conscious engagement and self-awareness, you, as a parent, can also grow. If you're willing to traverse to the dark side—the shadow, some call it—of your own heart and mind, and unearth aspects of yourself that may be uncomfortable and even nearly intolerable, new life can be brought to the surface. As a parent, you wish to be in control and to know it all; this helps you feel safe in this daunting endeavor of ushering the life of your precious child. However, it is often the most exasperating teen moments that can be the catalysts that open new spaces in the parental psyche.

Not only do you influence your teen by your very being, by your past, by your internal world, without saying a word, but they, in turn, influence you. As a mother, I have deep empathy for what it takes to be a parent in a way that feels useful to our children and sustainable and growth-enhancing for us.

Dostoevsky said that hell is the inability to love, and I agree. Witnessing the rancor and alienation of parents and teens, whose ties are so deep and potentially nourishing to one another, has a particular sting. Is it possible for members of our own family, our own children, to be so far removed from our emotional reach and even to be deeply destructive? Sadly, we all know that the answer is sometimes yes. There are two sides to this coin: those who love us can hurt us the most; those who love us are our most trusted healers.

The parent/teen relationship, *particularly the conflict*, is the opportunity for growth. This is what I have learned after nearly three decades of listening to lives unfolded before me, layer by layer. Taken together, some common themes emerge. I have distilled decades of listening and observation into seven transformational strategies that I have seen change lives. This book explains important theories about teen development, describes scenarios that cast light on common parent/teen problems, and offers exercises for developing a better under-standing of your teen and yourself. By employing the seven strategies, you can help resolve your teen's biggest problems *and* increase your experience of joy as a parent.

The connection between you and your teen requires a new lens. And you, as a parent, require new skills. This book outlines this dialectic process: the growth of your teen, how you create the space for this new birth, and how you change aspects of your self in order to stay connected to this new being. It's a tall order, being a parent of a teen. So this book is here for you.

This book is also intended to be a "limbic education" of sorts. The limbic part of our brain is responsible for the connection or attachment that makes mammals unique in the way that they rely so intimately and profoundly on each other. It is also responsible for the profound love, poetry, and mystery of the human relationship. The limbic system di-rects how mammals emotionally dance with and influence each other. This book is about how parents and teens must honor and understand this emotional dance or risk losing the most important bonds they have and also risk losing aspects of themselves.

What this ultimately means is that love—that deep human connection, the ability to know each other and be known—will always trump the pleasures of outward success or anything the brain can devise. It's just true. What matters is the quality of our human relationships and how they make us feel, whether our hearts are warmed, filled, joyous, or not. So why not figure out a way to really connect and stay connected to this precious being, your child, rather than get lost in the mire of pain and struggle? The latter is so easy to do!

These principles, based in the parent/teen dyad, describe profound findings about how parents and teens in particular affect each other. The relationship is not unlike other close, intimate bonds, but it has the particular stamp of the adolescent: rapid movements from childlike outbursts to mature philosophical clarity, from outrageous despair to exquisite hope, from a vague sense of where they left their backpack to a rock-solid set of beliefs that are their own creation. It's a dazzling ride! In these pages I offer "teen tips" for parents that I have collected through many years in academic, hospital, residential, and private practice settings, carefully observing what helps teens grow and thrive, and also how they fail. Healing is iterative and takes time, but it's worth the effort. Healing an alienated teen and their parent is the first step toward healing the collective wounds of the world.

The societal polarities that create suffering in our world—rich versus poor, black versus white, you versus me—are collections of broken bonds that often start in the first unit of human experience: the family. Thus, the most serious pain and the most sustained healing can often be delivered in the familial environment. Almost every political figure who has inflicted unimaginable pain on masses of people has also endured trauma and deprivation at the hands of their family. Unless a bond—a connection—exists, there is no incentive for human change. Thus, the wild seas of the parent-teen relationship provide an opportunity to change patterns on an intimate scale that can then reverberate to other relationships. If I am a mother whose anger at her teen becomes bitterness and separation rather than healing and reconnection, my role as a link in the chain of human-to-human love is lost.

It's important to note that while this is not a how-to book regarding parenting and technology, there is no question that technology is transforming the parent/child relationship. As we become more efficient—more like the computers on which we rely—how we retain what is uniquely and inexorably human and how we stay connected to our teens are questions that appear in the dilemmas parents and teens often face. We can only go so fast and still retain a connection to ourselves and to others. How to compete with the dopamine hit of the Instagram "follow"? Teens are technology natives; their parents, for the most part, are foreigners. What does this new technological revolution mean for love? And how do you connect with your teen, who is embedded in this environment, when you, no matter how much you embrace technology, are not?

I posit that we need to grow internally—emotionally and spiritually—as swiftly as we are living externally. So as we expand horizontally via the internet and the forces of globalization, we also need to go vertical: this involves pausing to think and feel, it involves meditation, and it involves understanding the role of one's own unconscious in relationships. I believe that just as there is a technology that governs the internet, our phones, and all things fast, so too is there a necessary process to slowing down and forging sustaining bonds with our children. We ignore these processes at our own peril. I am a devotee, in my personal and professional life, to limbic rhythms—those natural patterns of connection that mammals create that have become largely invisible in the fast world. These include presence, touch, meaningful communication, eye contact, hugs, and empathy. Families and our world require the safeguarding of these activities as our analog becomes digital and children become part of their devices.

We have to come to terms with this and many disjunctions and paradoxes about parenting today. This book will reveal and propose solutions for them. We need to find ways to connect with this world and the teen in it. Does your teen even know that she should slow down? The only way she will know is by the steady hand of a parent who is connected to herself and who knows the fruits of deep, sustained human connection. If you are alienated from your teen, they may be alienated from the human gems of this social fabric. And unless you embrace your teen emotionally, as they change and give birth to this new (and possibly, in our eyes, strange) creature of a self, you will fail to be their refuge. And we all know the value of refuge in times of great chaos and uncertainty.

Thus the ability to cultivate a connection with your teen, which requires inner work, is even more central in these times. They are embedded in the fast, perhaps less authentically connected world of technology, with little inspiration to do it any other way. Here's an analogy: your teen is on a train with all their friends. The train is going to a destination they will enjoy, and they're having a good time. But as they travel, they pass many places where, if they were to stop and have a picnic under a tree with you, other aspects of their being might have the chance to emerge. These aspects of self require more time and reflection and the perspective, history, and experience of someone who has been there, someone like you, can offer. This book is about making time to go visit that tree first by yourself, and then giving you the tools to be there with your teen. After all, if you are not connected to yourself, how can you expect anyone else, particularly your adolescent, to be connected to you?

I wrote this book as a kind of letter to myself and to all parents. We have precious little time to influence our children. As my own daughter rebels against me, she teaches me about my mothering challenges, like working too much and being in a chronic rush. Through her mirror, I see when I can pause and seek to grow in myself, whether that means slowing down, enjoying the moments with her, meditating, or revisiting my own childhood hurts. There are always significant rewards for both of us. When I see my therapist to work out my own emotional triggers—the ones only my daughter can elicit—I am giving her the greatest gift I can, which is my full presence as a human so that I do not have to unconsciously invite her to act out what I have decided not to face. None of this is an overnight, quick fix. But you know what they say about anything that's worthwhile? It takes time.

The philosopher Jiddu Krishnamurti wrote that "truth is a pathless land." These pages are a path of sorts, one marked by the paradoxes that lie at the heart of the parent/teen relationship and the truth that emerges when we can contemplate infinite possibility. Finding the details in enlarging the lens, letting go while holding on, and other practices will reveal the truth at the heart of your teen's journey and will inspire you to take a look at your own. The theories and encounters I describe are offered as a means of support for you and your teen to heal, grow, and find profound purpose in your relationship with each other.

Sometimes you need a guide so you can guide your teen. These strategies will encourage you to look in some possibly dark and fearful places while someone holds your hand. Some parents might learn how to let go of control and surrender. The mother who is self-critical and a perfectionist might need to see how she can tolerate imperfection in herself so that she can stop criticizing her teen and holding her to impossible standards. The father whose main coping mechanism is alcohol might come to understand that his son's marijuana addiction may not be solved if he continues with his own addictions. The mom whose body image is a bit shaky might learn ways to love herself so her teen can actualize her gifts and get over her obsession with her own body. The father whose unresolved grief makes him "inauthentic," according to his son, may have to face his own pain so as to have a renewed and satisfying relationship with his son and with himself.

I work with love lost: transforming broken ties between parents and teens first into connection and then into profound change for both. These pages reflect broken hearts and the medicine for mending them. My mission is to help you expand your soul—whatever that means for you—through moments of illumination, laughter, and tears. My hope is you will recognize yourself in my patients' struggles and achievements as they embrace grace, gratitude, and acceptance. And my belief is that if you open yourself to this journey, you will turn problems into gifts, love lost will become love found, and you will come to know that your teen is your teacher.

1

TRANSFORMATIVE STRATEGY #1:
ENDURE EMOTIONS

What is to give light must endure burning.

—Anton Wildgans*

T HIS IS A BOOK ABOUT THE TRUTHS THAT EMERGE
when we are willing to expand, to learn, and to grow in
the messiness. It's about the place where teens' troubles and
parents' growth converge, and both begin to see the world in
a different way. Your teen's conflict and the particular pain it
causes you can lead to either explosive outbursts and ultimate
stagnation or genuine change. The parent/teen relationship

---

*Anton Wildgans, "Helldunkle Stunde," *Mittag: Neue Gedichte* (Leipzig, Germany: L. Staackmann, 1917), 90, cited by Viktor Emil Frankl in *The Doctor and the Soul: From Psychotherapy to Logotherapy*, translated by Richard and Clara Winston (New York: Knopf, 1965), 67.

and the therapist/patient relationship are similar: both are crucibles in which heated activity has the capacity to produce great transformation. The heat that produces change lies in the emotional exchanges—sometimes the harmonious ones, but most often the challenging ones.

Ann came to me with concerns about her fourteen-year-old daughter, Jen, who was failing out of school and cutting herself. Jen had previously been diagnosed with attention deficit disorder; she was now exhibiting signs of depression. But as we peeled the layers back, I came to understand that Ann herself had issues around shame. Raised in a family rich in material wealth and poor in love and connection, Ann inherited a "false self" mantle that drove her to rely on external success and the pursuit of perfection in place of any authentic experience of self. As her daughter grew from a "good little girl," as Ann described her, to a challenging teen, Ann interpreted Jen's normal teen behaviors—oppositionalism, sass, moodiness—as a confirmation of Ann's failure as a mother. Because her sense of being good was so heavily dependent on all things outside of herself, including her children, she experienced what she saw as negative changes in her teen as *her* fault. Ann's own parents had been alcoholic and absent, so her conclusion in the midst of her daughter's challenges was that she herself was not worthy of love.

Shame is this consummate feeling of worthlessness. And shame is like the red wine stain on the white rug: it's tough to get out. Unlike guilt, which suggests that we feel bad about something we did, shame is about feeling that we are *essen-*

2

tially bad. It's the difference between "I did something bad" and "I *am* bad." So every time her daughter did something "bad," Ann felt the pain of her core wound: I *am* bad. This reduced her capacity to be helpful to her daughter and instead unleashed a powerful cocktail of anger and blame, which only drove her daughter further into despair—and further away from her mother, who should be her ally at this perilous time of her development. The core wounds of mother and daughter were colliding, and without illumination and strategies to heal, the consequences could be dire for both of them.

Ken Winters, a psychologist who specializes in working with adolescents, describes raising a teenager as dealing with someone whose emotions make them like a "child driving a Formula One race car."* Unfortunately, in order to experience positive emotions, we must also feel negative ones. They are all connected. That's why people who become very happy can also become very sad, whereas folks who stay somewhere around the middle tend not to be able to reach either the highs or the lows. Repressing emotions can have negative health consequences, because that denial leaves us without a compass with which to navigate our lives. Medicating our emotions with alcohol, sex, or other distractions may offer a short-term stay against pain, but they come with their own complications.

Studies have shown that suppressing emotions is actually unhealthier than was previously understood. Even if you

---

*K. C. Winters, "Alcohol and the Adolescent Brain: Tastes Great, Less Functioning," paper presented at the third Las Vegas Conference on Adolescents, Las Vegas, 2005.

successfully avoid contemplating a topic, your subconscious may still dwell on it. In a study from 2011, psychologist Richard A. Bryant and his colleagues at the University of New South Wales in Sydney told some participants, but not others, to suppress an unwanted thought prior to sleep. Those who tried to muffle the thought reported dreaming about it *more*, a phenomenon called "dream rebound."

Suppressing thoughts and feelings can even be harmful. In a 2012 study, psychotherapist Eric L. Garland of Florida State University and his associates measured a stress response based on heart rate in fifty-eight adults in treatment for alcohol dependence while exposing them to alcohol-related cues. Subjects also completed a measure of their tendency to suppress thoughts. The researchers found that those who restrained their thinking more often had stronger stress responses to the cues than did those who suppressed their thoughts less frequently.

So if just *not* thinking about our negative emotions and the things that provoke them doesn't work, what else can we do?

One common tactic for dealing with unwanted feelings is to project our emotions onto those around us—usually our spouse, our friends, or our children. As we soothe ourselves with the narrative of how someone else is the problem, we can count the ways they have wronged us, identify as the victim, or be in a constant rage about the indignities we've suffered because of other people. The problem with projecting as a way to handle emotions is that while it *does* do the job of protecting us against some of our pain, it also alienates the people with whom we wish to be closest.

4

We also know that the longer we have not faced an emotion, the more difficult it is to shift. One mother I worked with had never spent time alone in her life. She went from her parents' home to her husband's to having children, always finding safety in a very close connection to someone. This posed a problem when her twelve-year-old daughter, with whom she'd always been extremely close, started to show the normal signs of pulling away and spending more time with friends. Though she understood intellectually that her daughter needed to strike out on her own, on the inside she was experiencing profound feelings of anxiety and disorientation. So she found herself sending mixed signals to her daughter, flipping back and forth between complimenting her on her independence and making comments intended to make her daughter feel guilty for wishing to spend time with her friends instead of her mom. This woman was at a crossroads: either stifle her daughter's natural growth, or face what she perceived to be the unendurable loneliness that had lurked inside for her entire lifetime.

For many people, the idea of getting in touch with their feelings is at best unappealing and at worst a form of punishment. I call what I ask my clients to do "work" because it is. And like any effort worth undertaking, the work of feeling what is there to be experienced can yield great benefits. The dad of an eighteen-year-old admitted to a lifetime of suppressed emotion that he described as like the basement where you store all the stuff you don't want anymore. When his son attempted to speak to his father about his feelings, Dad said he went into a panic: it was as if he'd been asked to do something that was altogether impossible but that he knew was absolutely necessary. Clearing out the basement became a useful metaphor that invited Dad to take the project of getting to know his emotional world—his basement full of stuff—one emotion at a time. For most patients, feeling all the hurts and injustices at once is overwhelming; facing one's feelings is best done slowly, with a trusted person and in a safe environment.

The resistance to emotion can be subtle or deep, slight or profound. It can show itself in behaviors like parental anger and rigidity, or in depression and an inability to find empathy for our teen. Our unacknowledged stories can have an impact we won't even recognize until it's too late—like one mother who told me she'd essentially missed her daughter's childhood. "I just wasn't present," she said. Our resistance to knowing our own pain can also result in more dramatic experiences, like estrangement or ongoing conflict that feels like it has no resolution. If we are raised, for example, by narcissistic parents, we don't understand how to put our child first. So every need, demand, or challenge feels wrong or like an assault.

I tell the parents I work with that, unfortunately, no matter how emotionally depleted their own childhoods were, it is their job as the grown-up to rise to the occasion and take charge of the healing process. I don't let the teen completely off the hook either; the growth is in tandem. However, it is the responsibility of the adult to integrate complex emotional challenges and emerge on higher ground. Sorry for the bad news. But it's not all bad! And it's not all the parents' fault.

Our culture's stress on performance, outer appearances, and medicating any and all aberrations from "normal" feelings conspire to keep us sealed off from life. It's so much easier to go on another run, make another sale, buy another cute outfit, or have another drink of wine than it is to wade into the murky waters of our past pain and current inadequacies. But once we have exhausted all of our ingenious defense strategies, we are left with just one option: enduring our emotions. This is the key to substantial change inside us and inside our relationships. In the case of Ann and her daughter Jen, we had to start with the awareness that they were in something I call the Core Wound Dance. Teens and parents, married couples, or any two people involved in an intimate relationship will likely find themselves in this dance. We all have core wounds: vulnerable parts of ourselves usually from childhood that remain hidden until someone pokes at us a bit and then, suddenly, we are ten years old again and in the schoolyard fending off the bully, or home alone, frightened, waiting for our parents, who always worked late. Feelings from childhood that form our core wounds include experiences of loss, deprivation, and trauma. These wounds might be mild, such as a tendency to feel left out and thus withdraw. Or they might be severe, resulting in violent outbursts because of perceived threats to safety.

Some typical parent-teen dances include the angry teen and the parent with an inability to handle anger because of some overwhelming experience of aggression from someone in her past. Or the teen who lies to carve a sense of freedom and the parent whose sense of safety in the world relies on interactions based on the whole truth and nothing but the truth. Or the teen who pushes the parent away as a natural part of her development and the parent with a deep-seated fear of abandonment.

The reason this dance is so challenging is that our core wounds create unskillful and painful reactions to those we love. Reactions like anger, blame, and withdrawal separate us and fray the bonds of intimacy. As parents we need to maintain a strong connection with our teen and stay with them in the present as they cope with the challenges of their adolescence. But our wounds can act as static, interfering with that all-important two-way communication. Core wounds are part of our past and keep us from dealing with the present.

While I worked with Jen to give her awareness and tools with which to expand her expression of emotions so she could have outlets other than dangerous activities, I also invited Ann to endure the pain of the original wound. It was constant criticism and blame from her own mother that had predisposed Ann to feel ashamed. She began to understand that unless she could endure that original pain, sit with it, and through words and feelings metabolize it—just as we metabolize food in our digestive system to make good use of it in our bodies—she would continue to react to aspects of her daughter's behavior with blame, anger, and threats. Those kinds of responses would not make her daughter stop the unwanted behavior. Ann needed to develop empathy and deep listening in order to change her responses and move toward healing her relationship with her daughter. This is not an easy process. But moving *through* the pain, not around it, leads to transformation.

DEVELOPING THE REFLECTIVE CAPACITY

The ability to be responsive—to make conscious choices about our reactions rather than reactive ones—requires something that others have called "the reflective capacity."[*] The reflective capacity is the ability to pause and contemplate how an interaction makes us feel and what we can do in our own emotional state to change how we react to it. It includes behaviors such as examining one's own thoughts and feelings, remaining open and curious, and stepping back from the immediate intense emotion we are having to wonder what the experience means to our self and to our child. The reflective capacity is thwarted by an environment of judgment, criticism, and intolerance. It is helped in a relationship marked by trust, safety, and acceptance. Any process that turns an awareness toward our inner self—our thoughts, feelings, fears, unconscious emotions, and past wounding—will help build the reflective capacity. This capacity is particularly important when parenting a teen because their developmental directive to leap before they look and to live in action often gives us good reason to try to change *their* actions and look outside of ourselves for solutions.

For example, when a client's teenage daughter had her first fender bender, the mother's immediate fear-based reaction was

---

[*]Daniel J. Siegel and Mary Hartzell, *Parenting from the Inside Out: How a Deeper Self-Understanding Can Help You Raise Children Who Thrive* (New York: Tarcher/Penguin, 2003).

"No more car!" And who can blame her? As a parent we can understand this protective response. We want to keep our children safe at all costs. And yet part of a parent's job is to allow their teen to navigate appropriately challenging situations—like driving—to develop their autonomy. Sooner or later, if they are going to be a fully functioning member of our society, they are going to need to manage risk on their own.

Meditation is an excellent tool to develop the reflective capacity, as is psychotherapy or any other activity that soothes the nervous system and quiets the mind so our most adult and productive instincts can emerge. Simple strategies like noticing when you are flooded with emotion can provide opportunities for other positive interactions with your teen. For example, let's say your daughter is not responding to your text even though she said she would. Or your son's breath smells like marijuana and he's been driving. Or your daughter spoke to you rudely and will not emerge from her room. These are experiences that would understandably result in emotional flooding.

When you're flooded in moments like these, you might experience constricted muscles and rapid heartbeat and raise your voice when you speak. You might even experience feelings of dissociation—numbness or feeling that you're somehow outside yourself. These are adaptive when you were young and vulnerable as a child; they are not helpful as you navigate life with your teen. Intimate relationships can push you to a place where you are emotionally hanging onto the edge of the cliff for dear life. Cultivating a reflective capacity can support you in these moments to pause, listen inside, calm whatever feels out of control, and engage with your teen in a responsive rather than reactive manner. Thus, your interaction with your daughter who is not responding to her phone can be transformed from a shrill barrage of hysterical texts from you (which she will happily ignore) to a calm, effective communication with a clear directive and no hyper-emotional static. Your engagement with your son who has been smoking pot can become a quiet good night, rather than a fear-based monologue about his future homelessness peppered with threats. In the morning, when you and your son are both rested, you can initiate a thoughtful conversation about substance use, asking him how this use is likely to affect his future health and life goals, and inviting him to craft a solution for being responsible for his actions. Likewise, the irritation and abandonment you feel when your daughter just-a-little-too-rudely closes her bedroom door and asks to have dinner solo are quieted and transformed to connection-making overtures at other times.

To develop the reflective capacity in yourself, I encourage you to find ways to explore your own emotional territory, thoughts, feelings, hopes, and fears and to learn how to transform them to the benefit of yourself and your teen. One method that has helped many to develop their reflective capacity is to learn relaxation techniques.

WHAT DOES RELAXING HAVE TO DO WITH PARENTING MY TEEN?

In order to endure the mental and emotional roller coasters your teen often invites you to ride, you need a baseline of calm and stability. As life gets faster and busier and your children move from homebound tweens to roving teens, your ability to modulate your own mind and emotions is an essential aspect of good parenting. When you are tense or rushed, you are more likely to react from places of fear, anger, blame, and shame, which typically bring out the worst in your teen, who is ready for a power struggle at any provocation. When your body is in fight-or-flight mode, a nonrelaxed state, or your mind is distracted by multitasking, you do not have the ability to pause and think about the complicated scenarios your teen presents. States of tension like this often lead to snap reactions such as, "You're grounded for life!," "No more phone, ever!," or "What kind of human have you become?" These sorts of utterances do not pave the way for the collaborative connection that will most benefit you and your teen.

Research has found that practices such as yoga and meditation bring messages of relaxation to the brain. Science has validated the neurobiological benefits of meditation, which include a greater capacity to focus, accomplish tasks with more ease, and experience compassion for others. Quieting the mind and simple movements of the body increase the feel-good hormones oxytocin and prolactin, while decreasing the stress hormone cortisol. The exercises are not difficult to learn; resources like yoga classes and even apps can help you learn and practice. Some exercises involve a mere shift in your breathing. As a way to gain equanimity and balance in the midst of chaos, meditation is a core tool for parents of teens. Meditation practice reduces stress and allows for expansive thinking, which can act as a compass for navigating your teen's crisis-ridden situations. Meditation also helps us access what one of my teachers, Chris Griscom, calls the Higher Self, which is the part of our self that acts from love and wisdom rather than reacts from pain and fear.

Parents of traumatized teens can especially benefit from relaxation methods, which can help in developing the parents' capacity to manage their own nervous system. I have treated a wide range of teens in medical centers and in my private practice over the years: depressed, anxious teens suffering from post-traumatic stress; the "black sheep" of their family; the highly sensitive teens. In my work as the clinical director of a residential treatment program serving underserved and low-income teens, I learned about the behavioral and emotional consequences of trauma. Most of my patients, both parents and teens, suffer from some level of trauma, whether mild or severe. Mild trauma can result from negligent or inept but well-meaning parents, whereas more severe trauma stems from sexual and physical abuse, economic poverty, and other more chronic and intense insults to the growing psyche. The teens with more acute trauma come in with behaviors like cutting and suicidal feelings. Others seek a more authentic identity and experience a deep sense of isolation. Sometimes they're just a little rebellious or perfectionistic.

The word "patient" has at its root the Latin verb meaning "to suffer." All my patients are suffering, and all wish to feel better. And their parents are suffering with them. Parents need to cultivate internal space around this suffering *before* they can feel the important emotions that will allow for transformation.

EXERCISE: BREATHING MEDITATION TO INCREASE REFLECTIVE CAPACITY

Turn off your phone. Find a comfortable place to sit. Take a deep breath, and let it out slowly. Notice the sensation of the breath as it moves in and out of your nostrils. As you notice this sensation, your mind will continue to produce thoughts. Notice them—like clouds moving across the sky. And when you notice that your attention has moved to your thoughts, gently bring it back to the sensation of the breath as it moves in and out of your nostrils. It is natural for your mind to continue to generate thoughts. Just continue to gently bring your awareness back to your anchor, the sensation of the breath as it moves in and out of your nostrils.

If you find yourself feeling resistant to this exercise, and wanting to hurry on to the next section, it's even more important that you keep trying. Set a timer, and commit to doing this breathing exercise for just two minutes. That's all. You can do almost anything for just two minutes.

Reflecting on Your Experience of Meditation

What did you notice as you meditated? Were you comfortable? Uncomfortable? Did certain emotions arise? If you experienced difficulty, where was it? In your body? In your mind? Did you have recurrent thoughts? Thoughts that appear over and over can be considered the background noise of your mind. It's important to know what they are, because this kind of automatic thinking can keep us trapped in the same patterns. Did any of these thoughts pertain to fears about your teen? The more you meditate the more you'll become aware of the narratives that drive your behaviors. This awareness is crucial to having a relationship of growth, rather than a relationship of unconscious reaction, with your teen. Some common automatic thoughts parents have about their teens include the following:

> *I am afraid my teen will get hurt.*
> *I am afraid my teen will die.*
> *I am afraid my teen will fail.*
> *How can I get my teen to _____ ?*
> *My teen needs to _____ to be happy.*

Once you notice automatic thoughts, you'll be able to make choices about whether you act on those thoughts. One parent who was a recovering alcoholic was so convinced that her teen would become addicted to substances that alcohol-related stories (*my husband drinks too much; the parents at the school are too liberal with booze*) filled most of our sessions. Until this mom began to meditate and become aware of this persistent message in her own mind, she couldn't make the necessary changes to her own emotions and behaviors to allow her teen the possibility of making good choices.

Becoming familiar with the ways you block, deny, resist, medicate, or otherwise avoid emotions can make the difference between maintaining a relationship with your teen and becoming estranged. Your resistance to feeling your emotions can lead to interactions with your teen that result in their turning to peers or substances for connection rather than to you. Additionally, if your life as a parent is emotionally impoverished or restricted, your teen's world may be filled with slim connections instead of rich, rewarding ones.

So how do *you* use alcohol or other substances? Exercise? Anything you do compulsively is often a vehicle of avoidance. How do you know if it's compulsive? If someone suggested you go a week without a glass of wine, your phone, or that habitual late-night snack, would you panic? What you disavow or push away your teen will have to manage. Emotions are like children: they need our attention, or else they become unruly and unmanageable.

TEEN TIP 101: THE TEENAGE SOUL

Sometimes what you think is unbearable pain brought on by your teen's actions or attitudes is just the bitter pill you can benefit from swallowing. Feelings always seem unbearable until you bear them—and then you've moved to a new frontier. Adolescents need support from adults who cultivate their teens' ability to solve problems from the inside out. This doesn't mean that parents provide no guidance or wisdom. But as you move from a manager to a consultant, you invite your teen to examine their own thoughts, feelings, and values rather than adopting your ideas of what is right and rather than advising them on matters such as how much they should be sleeping, watching Netflix, studying, and so on. The more you purport to know your teen—"Maya is an athlete," "Mario needs at least nine hours of sleep," "Alma is a good student; she should capitalize on this strength"—the less room you give them for their own identity search. The more you swamp your teen with your theories or even factual data about living life rather than give them space for their own voice to emerge, the more likely they will ignore your input. Their process of self-discovery based on what I call "the calendar of the heart"—a slower, less linear, more internal, and emotionally based sense of time—should predominate over any externally imposed schedule. This pace and journey inward is their developmental rite. Ignore it at your peril.

In other words, your teen is in search of their soul. While we may not all share a definition of this word, if I asked my teen patients, most would nod, if tentatively, in agreement. Some teens in response to the question of soul seeking say it looks like more time to themselves to "do nothing." Others say they want to find a purpose that goes beyond schoolwork or their everyday routine. Usually this soul seeking involves pushing beyond a delineated idea of who they are into some unknown realm. The concept of the soul suits the teen's particular journey because it not only captures their developmentally appropriate sense of aspiration, growth, and adventure but helps parents appreciate the vastness of their teen's appetite for growth and the uniqueness of their teen's path.

Parents often become alarmed that their thirteen-year-old or fourteen-year-old has "lost interest" in things they used to love. While *doing* is important, the famous pediatrician Donald Winnicott observed that "boys and girls at puberty are . . . essentially concerned with being, with being somewhere, with feeling real, and with achieving a degree of object constancy. They need to be able to ride the instincts rather than be torn to pieces by them."* This means they often need a time-out from busy schedules, activities, and parent-driven ideas and ideals. As one thirteen-year-old reflected to me, "I just need some time and space to figure out how I feel about things in general. Everything seems different now and I'm just not sure about anything." Parents can become alarmed at this ambiguity, this sense of being lost or not living in a straight line. The language of the teen is ambiguous so as to create space for her identity to emerge—so as to create a sense of infinite possibility. As Carl Jung himself put it: "The language I speak must be ambiguous, must have two meanings, in order to do justice to the dual aspect of our psychic nature. I strive quite consciously and deliberately for ambiguity of expression, because it is superior to unequivocalness and reflects the nature of life."†

Teens require space and the tolerance of ambiguity. (Raise your hand if this sounds familiar: "I thought you said you

---

* D. W. Winnicott, *Home Is Where We Start From: Essays by a Psychoanalyst* (New York: W. W. Norton, 1986), 25.

†C. G. Jung, *Selected Letters of C. G. Jung, 1909–1961* (Princeton, NJ: Princeton University Press, 1984).

would be at the restaurant, so why did you end up at Sally's house?") Teens need to be able to make their own decisions— with their parents' guidance, of course—and to have the time for reflection, to become their own people.

In her insightful book *The Price of Privilege*, Madeline Levine chronicles the struggles and stresses of adolescents who are so programmed and overshadowed by their parents that their own identities are muted. The teens Levine describes struggle to find authenticity or a modicum of happiness because, among other factors, their well-meaning parents lack the capacity to encourage both internal and external spaciousness for their teens.

You can help your teen cultivate internal spaciousness when you pull back from attempts to control them, limit your projections, and give your teen authority over the development of their own internal world. What this means in practice, of course, is managing daily exchanges with the goal of internal spaciousness in mind. Say your daughter suddenly wants to wear only black and get piercings and a tattoo. Your immediate reaction is fear and anxiety. But if you want to encourage her to develop her own good judgment, you will have to move from boss to consultant to stay in conversation with her.

By external spaciousness, I mean allowing the teen the time and space to just *be*. This might require reducing a frantic schedule and celebrating boredom. It might mean sitting with your fear about piercings—and addressing them calmly *after* you've processed it. By giving your teen the gift of free time and space, you allow them a canvas for healthy experimentation.

TRANSFORMATION IN PRACTICE: LILY'S STORY

Here's an example of how parents endured the pain of their own past to liberate their daughter from perfectionism. Lily, a teenager, came to me with chronic abdominal pain and paralyzing panic attacks that kept her from school and all other normal activities for a few months. Her family history was clear of any significant anxiety disorders, and her parents didn't understand what was causing her attacks. Like many parents, Laura and John believed that working hard was an important component to future success. While they were kind and nonauthoritative parents, their own anxiety about failure and falling below a middle-class status had been subtly transferred to their daughter, who couldn't sleep at night because of anxiety. This points out the power of her parents' quiet, unconscious, unspoken, but not-so-subtle communication.

Laura and John espoused balance and didn't overtly push Lily to achieve, so the pressure she felt was subtle because she had internalized the message of success or bust. We call it "ego-syntonic" when perfectionism and success orientation—or any attitude that causes undue anxiety—is unconscious to those who experience it. A person may experience anxiety but not identify it as such. Laura and John weren't even aware of their own unconscious fears about success. Like fish swimming in water, they thought that their pressurized way of living was the only way. Children, however, are sensitive to subtle messages and can pick up on these signals, as Lily did.

This is where the transformative strategy of enduring our emotions applies. Like many parents in my practice, Laura and John earnestly denied putting pressure on their daughter. It took a number of sessions to uncover the deeper narrative of fear of failure and the black-and-white thinking related to how the world works. John would exclaim with a sense of absoluteness, "In this world you're either the player or you're the ball." While his ideas may have some validity, they didn't allow for his daughter's own experience of life, and the anxiety behind them was making her ill.

Words cannot reverse this. It's not enough to say, "Relax, it will all be okay." Children do what we do, not what we say. When I met with Lily's parents, they told me, "We just don't want Lily to have to work as hard as we do, with two jobs, making very little money." Lily, naturally bright and motivated, did well in school. She felt she needed to be perfect to ease her parents' anxiety. This projected anxiety then became internalized and now was nearly impossible to eradicate.

Feeling Your Feelings

One way to heal perfectionism is to invite those experiencing it to experience failure. This isn't easy, especially in a culture that so lavishly rewards perfect outcomes. Lily and her parents were terrified to be anything less than perfect. But when we avoid failure, our symptoms of anxiety actually *increase*. So to ease perfectionism, we must feel our feelings.

In Lily's case, the first step was for her parents to learn to meditate—to create space for their feelings. After a few months of regular meditation practice, in addition to our therapy sessions, Laura had a more acute awareness of how her expectation of perfection—for herself and for her daughter—dominated most of her thinking. Awareness is the first step in any change process. John, after a similar period of meditation and therapy, was able to identify the feelings that fueled his anger toward his daughter: they were rooted in his own fears of inadequacy and his wish to prevent Lily from suffering the way he had, growing up poor. Lily's parents realized that their expectations of Lily were based in their own previously unconscious experiences of themselves. Equipped with this awareness, they were better able to slow down their internal narrative and even change behaviors. Laura found herself spending more relaxed time with Lily, and Lily in turn felt closer to her mom, and thus more motivated to listen to Laura's requests. John and Lily, whose relationship had become significantly strained as a result of his anger, started to heal as Lily experienced her dad as calmer and more understanding of her struggles.

The second step was to uncover and understand the deeper streams of anxiety they were experiencing. Her father was quick to anger when he heard Lily wasn't "doing her best." While this phrase is common and well-intentioned, most teens who are prone to anxiety or perfectionism cannot make good use of it because they never know exactly what "their best" means.

I invited Lily's parents to assess—from a deep place and over a number of sessions—their own paradigm of success. Hard work can be an important aspect of success. But when anxiety clouds a child's functioning, creates a chronic scowl, and creates burnout by age fifteen, before the truly long haul of adulthood has even begun, the child will not have the tools she needs for long-term success. Even though Lily's mom and dad assured me that they never verbally pressured their daughter, she was picking up the message.

How could this be? Only 10 percent of what people communicate to others is transmitted verbally. The other 90 percent is transmitted nonverbally. In unconscious ways, you can communicate to your child a focus on working yourself to the bone, competing with your peers, and ultimately reducing your capacity for joy. This transfer of anxiety happens quietly and over years of well-meaning encouragement.

As Lily's parents developed an awareness of their attitude toward success through cognitive examination and somatic experiencing of their own childhood wounds, Lily's anxiety diminished. In this process, as Lily and her parents became more free to choose their relationship to work and success rather than being driven by old stories, their connection to each other also grew stronger. Lily revealed that she felt she was seeing her parents with new eyes and found herself seeking their company rather than shutting them out to protect herself from their nervous questions about her life.

Emily Dickinson famously wrote, "To live is so startling it leaves little time for anything else." These words couldn't be more true about life with teens. Their capacity for and interest in feeling—in soulful seeking—is increased and exaggerated. So if you wish to remain in contact with your teen— which is highly advised both for your satisfaction and for their health—you need to start living in relationship with this new being. This means expanding your own capacity to live, feel, and know yourself deeply. It is not enough just to think, "My teen is making me sad." You need to understand *where* that sadness lives in relation to your own history and your own present. You need to learn how to work with that sadness so it is not projected onto your teen and does not become a chronic stance that they will ultimately imitate. This is no easy task. Let's dive into an exercise that will help you take the first steps toward deeper knowing.

EXERCISE: KNOW YOUR PERSONAL TRIGGER MAP

Triggers are incidents or interactions with people in our environment that bring out unresolved feelings. Our teens trigger us! If we are unthinkingly engaged in our teen's rebellious, moody, power-seeking or otherwise triggering behaviors, the relationship *will* deteriorate. A Personal Trigger Map is a simple tool that brings us awareness of our most sensitive triggers. Here are some questions that will guide you to your Personal Trigger Map:

- What upsets you most about your teen? Does it remind you of anyone (mother, father, sibling) in your past?
- What is your style of reacting to theses triggers? Do you withdraw? Explode? Play the victim? Lecture? Control? These are just some of the coping styles many parents have.
- What do you secretly fear about yourself? How does this affect your reactions to your teen?

THE PARADOX AT THE HEART OF IT ALL

Teens demand that we set limits and allow them freedom. This is a paradox. As you learn to endure your emotions, you'll be able to surrender appropriately to the changing adolescent who is one moment an adult living in your home and the next a child curled up in your bed. Developing the capacity to tolerate two seemingly opposing activities is crucial to approaching your teen's complex dilemmas with clarity.

For example, how do you deal with lies? Lying is a common form of distancing and finding one's identity that teens employ, but even if you know that, it's normal to feel let down or even threatened when your teen lies to you. How do you communicate that deceit is wrong and that you wish for more honest communication?

The more neutral, curious, and nonjudgmental we are about our teens' behaviors, even lying, the more influence we can wield to help them cultivate positive behaviors. To create this place of equanimity in the face of our teens' most challenging behaviors requires us to go inside ourselves and feel. Jung notes "what we resist persists." I believe these resistances persist both in ourselves and in our teens.

Many of the parents I work with understandably believe that honesty is a fundamental aspect of their family life. I invite them to understand the developmental meaning behind lying or omitting the truth so that they can respond appropriately and not fan the flame of what I call the trust-mistrust cycle. In a nutshell this cycle has the following stages: teen betrays your trust; you react strongly and do something draconian like take away their phone for a month; they stop listening to you and escalate the out-of-control behaviors. And the cycle repeats. The most valuable solutions emerge when you learn to process paradox within yourself and outside of your interactions with your teen.

The more you can entertain paradox and practice the art of holding two seemingly opposing emotions in order to produce something valuable, the better you'll be at interacting with your teen. Entertaining paradox is akin to tolerating ambiguity. For example, you are seething inside because your teen deceived you about her whereabouts—again. *And* (not but!) you know that she was trying to assert her own independence and was not in any actual danger, and the lie had to do with the ultimately fairly harmless situation of being at one restaurant rather than another. As you listen to your teen defend their lie, you hold two opposite feelings: anger at being deceived and desire to support her growth. You're in the ambiguous zone: you're not all good, and your teen isn't all bad. You experience both your own disappointment, your wish to remain connected to your teen, and you also consider the nuances of your teen's desires and behaviors.

There's a Chinese proverb that says, "Our children need roots and wings." How do you stay fearless and face your emotions while still setting appropriate limits, so that both you and your teen can face challenges and grow? In other words, how do you help them find both roots *and* wings? Successfully answering this question will keep you and your teen thriving rather than suffering in confusion.

EXERCISE: ENDURING YOUR EMOTIONS

This exercise will help you put the pieces of this chapter together by helping you understand your own feelings, relate them to your teen, and ultimately determine a strategy for enduring your emotions.

- Name one feeling that you are resisting that may be blocking your ability to be present with your teen.
- Name one problem your teen is having that may relate to your incapacity to feel an uncomfortable feeling.
- Be honest about your interest in connecting with your teen. What is your desire? What are you actually doing to create or allow this connection?
- Commit to one daily practice, such as meditation or identifying triggers, that will increase your capacity to *feel* discomfort and thereby grow.

Your growth through your teen's challenges is an evolutionary imperative; children unconsciously wish to heal their parents' deepest wounds. They will not let their parents continue in their egotistical madness! Healthy connections prevent stress. The more pain you are in right now, the more desperately the message from within must be heard.

Can you trust the first step of this process?

Can you endure the possibility of enduring?

2

TRANSFORMATIVE STRATEGY #2:
ENLARGE THE LENS

W HEN YOUR TEEN CHALLENGES YOUR SENSE OF trust, you may be tempted to ground them for life. Even if you don't go that far, your fears may limit their potential in other, even unforeseen ways. But sometimes it's helpful to stretch in the opposite direction to give your teen the message that you trust them—even in the midst of their mistakes. This chapter is about attempting to see the bigger picture when you're mired in the petty details. It's no easy task.

Developmentally, teens need their parents to find the right balance between close contact and leaving them alone. This is why the ability to enlarge the lens is even more crucial for teens than it is for your younger children. Teens absolutely demand your ability to give them space! And if you don't give it freely, they will take it in ways that may be dangerous. A colleague likens this stance of being present yet appropriately distant to hanging out at the side of the pool. You are in the pool, you can see your child, but you are at the edges, not right beside them. After all, they're never going to learn how to swim if you are always there, holding them up. By being close yet giving them space, you are allowing them to experiment and make mistakes. But you are also a heartbeat away should they call for help or start to drown.

Teens know how to push your buttons. She used to be your best friend. Now she's mean and sullen and sometimes she even calls you the B-word. Your sweet son, who used to love to bake, now won't stop playing shoot-'em-up computer games. And he's smoking pot. Or maybe your teen is fine, but you're still worried all the time, and it's pushing you to the edge.

One dad who came to my office was particularly concerned—angry, in fact—that his seventeen-year-old high school senior had been caught repeatedly leaving the school campus without telling his teachers or parents. While Dad was triggered—"College prep time is no time for goofing off!"—I invited him to see the bird's-eye view of his son.

His son was a strong student, a kind and responsible boy with a good head on his shoulders who was needing physical space from the pressures of high school. Dad—who came from a family that had dissolved in divorce and for whom being close meant knowing exactly what was going on moment to moment with his family—was reactive and angry when the school called and said they didn't know where his child was during a free study period.

As it turns out, his son would drive down the road to a field, where he would walk and just let his mind wander. Dad's fear-based, small view resulted in anger: "We don't leave the school premises; these are the rules." He held onto this tightly because of his own need for knowing where his child was. But the expanded view looks beyond the narrow rules to include the whole child, their history, what you know to be true about their character, and your awareness of your own emotional reactions that are based in your past. The dad's restricted lens was hyper-focused on the present situation and all the details and fears triggered by his son's leaving campus without permission. But the bird's-eye view saw his son's needs as a person at this stressful time and invited a suspension of Dad's own need to know so that he could allow his son the necessary space to navigate his senior year and the normal growth that was under way.

Parents are the keepers of their teen's physical, emotional, and overall life success. That's a big job, and as such, it's easy to become fixated on the details but lose sight of both your own larger life patterns and ultimate goals as well as those of your teen. Whatever the specific details, your desire to make things better, to fix your child's problem, is always a factor, as is your fear that it will only get worse.

LOVE AND FEAR

There are two core emotions: love and fear. All others derive from these, more or less. Enlarging the lens means choosing love over fear. Love requires expansion, and fear is the opposite of expansion. Physiologically, fear constricts our muscles and can dysregulate our heartbeat, and mentally, it narrows our reasoning capacities. Interacting with your teen from a place of fear brings out the worst in them. Love, on the other hand, opens up both body and mind and creates a fertile ground for communication with your child.

When fear is unwarranted—which it often is—it inspires mistrust and distance between you and your teen. The amount of time you spend fretting and creating disaster scenarios starring your teen is likely far greater than the true amount of time your fear needs to be engaged to protect your teen from danger.

Love expands, includes, and tolerates. Love requires an absence of fear. Love manifests as gratitude, acceptance, ease, and joy. The good news is that our minds are powerful. New research in psychoimmunology—the science of mind-body medicine—reveals that our mind can heal cancers and transform every system of the body, including the nervous system, the immune system, and the endocrine system. So your mind can actually help you manage your relationship with your teen.

Raising children with as little fear as possible in perilous times is no easy task. This is why I wrote this guide. Because when the outside world is telling you that the sky is falling, it's even more important that you examine the emotions that drive your decisions. Otherwise, you might end up raising children who can no longer make the distinction between fear and love.

EXERCISE: VISUALIZATION
TO ENLARGE THE INNER SPACE

This is an exercise that engages both your conscious mind and the subtle aspects of your "vibe," if you will. When we practice bringing our mind's power and all that is unconscious or invisible to us—thoughts, feelings, subtle energies—to the surface, so we can be aware of them, we support both our teen's and our own growth. This practice, adapted from my studies with Chris Griscom, also supports decision making from a deeper, larger-lensed, and more aware place as it reduces reactivity and fear. Let's give it a try.

Find a comfortable place to sit. Breathe deeply, into your belly. Imagine you are sitting inside an orb, a glowing ball. Choose a color that you find to be soothing or empowering, whatever state you wish to engender. Take a moment to ask your Higher Self, that non-fear-based self, what it wishes that part of you to embody. Then breathe that color into that space—the orb around you. Imagine you are drawing that color from above you down *into* your body and then out your solar plexus.

Sit and breathe.

Continue to energize this field with this color for a few minutes.

Now imagine any dilemma you are currently facing with your teen, big or small. Or even just an old fear that seems to be hanging on. Whatever it is, bring this dilemma or concern into your awareness while keeping that visual of the color field surrounding you. Can you feel a difference in how you see the situation?

When you enlarge your inner space, the issue becomes smaller. You can then bring a calmer and more secure self to your interactions with our teen. This is the self our teen needs us to find in order to be large enough to address the turmoil they face.

> Do you know what you are?
> You are a manuscript of a divine letter.
> You are a mirror reflecting a noble face.
> This universe is not outside of you.
> Look inside yourself;
> Everything that you want,
> You are already that.*
>
> —Rumi

TRANSFORMATION IN PRACTICE:
RESISTING THE WORST-CASE SCENARIO

Tina came from a family of alcoholics and was always worried about what would happen when her teens began experimenting with substances. So when she got the call that her

---

*Jalal al-Din Rumi, *Hush, Don't Say Anything to God: Passionate Poems of Rumi*, translated by Shahram Shiva (Fremont, CA: Jain Publishing, 1999).

daughter Terry, age fifteen, had passed out in the park and was now at the police station, her anxiety went through the roof. She had a panic attack and was ready to fast-forward to rehab for Terry.

By Tina's own description, her daughter was an otherwise successful, happy, level-headed teen. Terry was experimenting very mildly with alcohol, and this was one of her first ventures—a typical live-and-learn situation. To be clear: the danger of teens and substance abuse shouldn't be minimized, but Tina's reaction was out of proportion and counterproductive. She wanted to lock Terry in her room for the next four years.

Her daughter reported to me in a later session that when her mom got upset and didn't trust her, it made her want to do "bad things more" just to show her that she, not her mom, was in charge of her life. According to Terry, when her mom was able to stay calm, Terry wasn't afraid to be honest with her.

After a few sessions with Tina, we were able to identify her fundamental wounding—the matrix of painful and maladaptive emotions and relational habits that brought her to therapy. As a child, Tina had dealt with the lack of structure created by her parents' alcoholism by maintaining a very tidy life in which she controlled everything. Though she was now an adult and a mother herself, this "out of control" behavior by her teen was rattling to the little girl inside, who was alone and had no adults to let her know it was going to be okay.

Remarkably, this incident enabled Tina to actually free up parts of her life that had been stuck for years. She was able to speak in an open and nonpunishing way to Terry about her concerns, and create rules around substance use.

In turn, her daughter was able to listen to her mom and respond by agreeing to text Tina more frequently for the next few months as she regained her trust. Tina was able to see both the big picture of her daughter—who was actually a responsible young woman—and the big picture of her own life, in which she recognized that her inner child needed to come out of her rigidly organized world.

This incident was the catalyst for great expansion in the mother-daughter relationship. With the level of fear that Tina's inner child had experienced for years, a broad and bird's-eye conversation like this would never have been possible without something to push them over the edge. But now, rather than recoiling in fear and resorting to more control of her daughter, who was pushing for trust and freedom, Tina was able to have candid, non-fear-based conversations with her daughter about substance abuse, behavioral choices, and more.

The first step toward identifying your own inner child is to turn inward and pay attention to the extreme reactions you have to your teen—anger, fear, sadness, and even positive extremes like hope and expectation. Often these reactions are the sum of early experiences and emotions. The inner child is a metaphor and tool for identifying this set of primitive or early emotions; listening to this part of you with your adult self is part of the solution. Next time your teen triggers you, invite your inner child to the table. What age is she? What is she wearing? What is her mood? What need is she bringing to the adult part of you for acknowledgment and healing? This work is best done in the context of psychotherapy, as it can be difficult to identify these deep places on our own. But an awareness of this process can begin the journey.

EXERCISE: GETTING TO THE GIFT

From my work with thousands of teens, I have come to believe that parents and teens have a particular purpose that can only be found in their relationship with each other. And usually the toughest part about appreciating the larger purpose of why their teen came to them lies in looking at the painful parts.

How might you summarize, in one or two sentences, the unique relationship you have to your teen? Think about how your growth is enhanced by your teen's unique characteristics or behaviors. Here are some examples:

"I cultivate calm and harmony so I can relate to my intense and spirited daughter with enjoyment and success."

"I stay in contact with the shame experienced by my inner child so I don't overreact and shame my son when he engages in developmentally appropriate behaviors that I might deem disrespectful."

"I am cultivating a relationship to the deeper current of my emotions, rather than living on the surface, so my teen doesn't have to invite me into intensity with dramatic acts like cutting or other self-harming behaviors."

As you move through this chapter, I challenge you to stay engaged with this question: What part of your Higher Self— the non-fear-driven, love-based side of you—is pushing to emerge in relationship to your teen's most perilous behaviors or challenging emotional experiences?

TRANSFORMATION IN PRACTICE: SALLY'S STORY

When David, Sally's father, came to see me, he recoiled in disgust at her social-butterfly approach to life. "All she cares about is her friends. It's ridiculous," he would often say in our sessions. While his observation that Sally's social engagements were dominating her time to the exclusion of all else had some truth to it, the emotional lens and judgment—the disgust, the labeling as "ridiculous"—were based in his own fears. Not only was his attitude distancing and unhelpful, it also led David to overlook Sally's significant social gifts and see the larger stage on which those gifts might benefit her.

Sally had a natural magnetism based in a sense of humor and an empathy for others that was stunning and unusual. The range of friendships she had—from the geeks to the jocks to the kids who had few friends—suggested a truly special gift for connection and empathy. She also volunteered in a homeless shelter because she wanted to understand people who were struggling. This appetite for connection and the experience of humanity was not well supported by her father when he reduced it to something to be criticized or even ridiculed.

As with most of the challenges teens present, there is usually something behind parents' powerful reactions that merits deeper analysis. For David, his concerns were that Sally's socializing would prevent her from succeeding in other areas. In further examining his fears, we unearthed strong feelings about his own mother, who had destroyed her own life and the life of her family by abandoning them to pursue a life of high society socializing to the detriment of those she loved. He was determined to never be the victim of this type of experience again, and his view of his daughter's much more balanced socializing was eclipsed by his painful past. After identifying this distortion, I invited him to look at the ways that these relationship skills could ultimately serve Sally and the people around her. He was able to have a more open, less judgmental view of her friend- and people-focused life, and he and Sally found common ground about balancing her social life with scholastic and other nonsocial endeavors.

EXERCISE: CHALLENGING THE NARRATIVE

First, write down a sentence or two about one aspect of your child that irritates or concerns you. For example, "My child does the minimum amount of work to get by" or "My son is a star athlete with little regard for grades" or "My daughter is an accident waiting to happen, a bull in a china shop." Then, create a narrative as complete as possible by adding sentences describing your feelings about that concern, the circumstances that surround it, and what you do in response. The more you know about the context of these reactions, the better able you will be to skillfully manage them.

This narrative is based on assumptions and ideas you have about your teen, and it drives how you behave toward them. While there may be some facts or truth behind the narrative you've created, your assumptions do not allow you to see *all* of who our teen is, neither the full person now nor the potential adult. So the next step is to challenge those assumptions: see the bigger picture, and rewrite the narrative with an approach that allows for growth and change in your child. For example, "My child does the minimum amount of work to get by" might be expanded with ". . . so she can do what she truly loves, which is creating stories and characters that entertain people."

FEELING THE PAIN OF SEPARATION FROM OUR TEEN

Another activity that enlarges the lens and improves our relationship with our adolescent is navigating the separation process. For most parents, stepping away and giving their teen more space to grow into himself doesn't come naturally. "She treats me like I'm eight," one seventeen-year-old opined. Enlarging the lens to include not only the teen's pushes and pulls but also the parent's own feelings of loss and separation is a necessary aspect of parenting. In my practice, I find that parents who cannot feel these feelings create stress in themselves and in their relationship with their children. Jack and James were one such pair.

Jack had become intensely uncomfortable with the behavior of James, his teenage son. James was spending more time with friends and less time with his parents, engaging in what his Dad felt to be "unproductive" behavior and spent more time in his room to "chill and be alone." Jack's alternately angry and cloying behavior in response to his son was only driving James away, which further reduced any impact he hoped to have on his son's life.

There was a further problem: Jack could not tolerate his son's emotionality. Boys are already given an impoverished education when it comes to emotional skillfulness, awareness of self, and the ability to be vulnerable. So when a dad like Jack insists that his son "man up," it's a serious setback.

A few sessions with Jack revealed that he was anxious because of his own upbringing. He had never properly separated from his parents, so he was using his son as a quasi-parent figure, relying on him for emotional needs that he couldn't meet himself. Once Jack finally allowed himself to feel his unmet needs from childhood, and to acknowledge this vulnerable, younger side of himself, communication with his son was much improved. The father had to feel the pain of his own separation from his parents in order to give his son the necessary space to grow up.

In speaking with James, it was clear that he had begun to use marijuana as a way to numb his confused feelings of guilt related to pushing his dad away and sensing his dad's sadness at being pushed away. Jack later joked about "breaking up" with his son—referring to the invisible bond that was responsible both for the love and goodness between them but also for the enmeshment that was interrupting the son's natural separation process. I would joke, "Breaking up is hard to do!" This is the kind of bond I usually see with mothers and eldest daughters. But it can happen with fathers and sons, as well as any other combination of parent and teen.

After we righted Jack's inner child a bit, James felt much freer to be himself, and his guilt vanished. So did his marijuana use. Jack and James were a great example of a parent and teen willing to do the work. By allowing themselves to feel uncomfortable feelings and come to terms with their own enmeshment, they were able to stop clashing.

Parents and teens get tangled together. This is part of the joy *and* the pain. When each has unconscious issues that remain hidden, these issues intersect and create worse problems. These matrices can put parents and their teens on a path of pain that is difficult to heal. The goal is to jointly see these dilemmas and find the path out.

EXERCISE: MEDITATION TO MOVE TOWARD THE CENTER OF ONE'S SELF

Your relationship with your teen relies on an authentic connection with them and an equally authentic connection with yourself. When you're out of balance, either triggered by your teen or unable to separate yourself from their struggles, you can feel lost. This can lead to communication breakdowns with your teen. Here's an exercise to find your way back to yourself. Even if you don't believe in a higher power, I urge you to give this exercise a chance.

Breathe.
Draw the breath down into your lower belly. Slow it down. Feel the stillness beginning to surround your body. Feel yourself grounded, sending a cord from your

feet to the center of the earth. You are going on a journey inward.

Now imagine that you are walking in a spiral until you begin to see a beautiful little garden in the distance.

As you come close to the center, you see steps leading up to the garden. You go up the steps and enter into a space of exquisite beauty and immense peace. You go to the center of the garden and sit. You notice your body relaxing even more, and you feel the overwhelming love that dwells here. You have always known this place, yet it feels as if you are experiencing it for the very first time. This is the home of your soul. There is no fear here—only peace.

I want you to imagine that a Spirit is now in your midst. You feel the profound love of this Spirit. Your body is fully at ease. Your mind is quiet. Your emotion is joy. You have arrived home.

Let the love of this Spirit touch you. It reaches your fear, your sadness, your sense of separation.

When you're ready, slowly get up from where you're sitting in the garden. Walk down the steps and into the spiral, and slowly walk it again in reverse, until you return to where you started.

FATHER AND CHILD

Doug, a well-meaning but emotionally cut-off programmer, was struggling to understand his daughter's suffering. "Emotions are a bit foreign to me," he said. He went on to recount reactions that I have found to be more typical of my male patients because of the conditioning they receive to disavow emotions at a very young age. "I go into fight-or-flight mode," he told me, revealing his vulnerability and providing insight into his own challenges. "I know I shouldn't get mad and grab her iPhone, but I'm so worried and pissed, I just don't know what else to do. I want to trust her; she's a good kid. But she knows we have certain standards and expectations, and I feel she's just flipping me the bird by ignoring me and going to her room."

Mothers and fathers are both susceptible to reactivity. On the whole, as Freud predicted, I find that fathers are more susceptible to concerns about performance and failure in the real world. They often react from places of their own shame and inadequacy through sarcasm or veiled (and sometimes not-so-veiled) anger.

In a joint session with Doug's daughter Sarah, she explained, with eyes pleading to be understood: "I'm home in bed, sick with depression, and my dad has no idea what to say. I could be suicidal, not sure. I have loads of plans. Most obvious is slitting my wrists. But then I could also jump out a window, hang myself. . . . There's a rope lying around that might do." She has ramped up the stakes for her dad's benefit; maybe then he can hear her?

Your teen might not be as explicit about communicating their distress, but in ways both subtle and obvious, with their words or with their actions, our teens are talking to us all the time. Are you listening?

MOTHER AND CHILD

Pam faced a challenge that more of my female clients are susceptible to. A wonderful, devoted mother of three teenagers, she became depressed when all three of her teens entered the "rejecting Mom" phase simultaneously.

The truth is that by the time children reach adolescence, many parents are ready for a change. Some are interested in a career change, some wish to travel, some are ready to begin dating again, and so on. But after so many years of putting their children first, sometimes parents repress these desires—or worse, try to live through their teen—with the result that both parent and child feel stifled and unhappy.

In order to enlarge the lens, you must have your own life. This may mean work, volunteering, or gardening. Mothers who are hyper-focused on their children are often bored or using energy that they could be using to keep their own selves and lives balanced. This doesn't mean that stay-at-home moms can't have a healthy distance from their teens. But I have found that mothers who have a well-developed life outside of their parenting role tend to be able to see the bigger picture more easily and bring the wisdom from their other endeavors to bear on life with their teen.

In the case of Pam, she found that returning to work turned out to be the best way for her to avoid power struggles with her teens. As your child moves through adolescence, it's a good time to ask yourself: What have you been longing to do? Who have you been longing to be?

DISTRACTION

We live in a time when using the mind in endlessly scattered ways is touted as high-level multitasking that will supposedly "get us somewhere." But the truth is that hopelessly divided attention simply leads to distraction, and distraction is a common issue for many of the parents and teens I work with. Distraction diffuses your energy and sends the message to your teen that whatever is flashing across your phone or computer screen is more important than they are.

As you look at your role in generating a field of potentiality both for your teen and your *relationship* with your teen, you would be wise to examine subtle energetic practices, like gratitude, mindfulness, visualization, and identifying hopes and dreams. Ideally, both the conscious and unconscious messages your teen is receiving from you will support them to grow into their best self.

EXERCISE: ELIMINATING DISTRACTIONS

Identify one distraction in your life that keeps you from your internal world, from knowing your feelings, and also from spending the time you wish to spend with your teen. Can you think of a way to reduce your engagement with this distraction? Maybe it's putting your phone on silent and facedown when your teen is talking to you. Maybe it's creating a time of the day where work ends, no matter what. Whatever it is, make one promise to yourself about how you will reduce your engagement with this distraction for one week, and then keep track of any feelings, conversations, or challenges this newly opened space provides.

DILEMMAS

Your hidden emotions will present themselves as dilemmas with your teen. Understanding what you are hiding is another way of expanding the lens. Parents often spend sleepless nights asking questions such as, "How much freedom should I allow? How upset should I have been when he stayed out way past his curfew? What about those hickeys—is she ready to have a boyfriend?" While answering these questions is important, usually when you are unable to solve a dilemma, the problem is larger than the simple facts at hand.

Expanding the lens first requires acknowledging that these dilemmas, like all dilemmas, have at least two sides. Additionally, when you are obsessing about a problem and answers seem elusive, underlying emotions are often what keep the mind stuck. With your teen, the fear that there are no solutions, or that your teen will never listen to you even if you propose one, adds fuel to the frenzied mind's inability to lock onto an answer. The realization that for some of these dilemmas your teen needs to take the lead can also be a difficult experience to accept—thus keeping you in search of an easier solution, like going back to the days when you were in control. Or maybe your son's normal experimentation with alcohol and your inability to come up with a plan reveal your fears that he will become like alcoholic Uncle Charlie, who lost everything and was disowned by the family. Maybe the hickeys on your daughter's neck, while triggering your worst fears based on your own challenging teen years, are part of her natural experimentation with affection, and rather than condemnation, she needs a conversation. Unlocking these hidden emotions and expanding the lens can clarify your goals for your teen and help you see the situation for what it is, rather than trying to solve for something that it isn't.

TRANSFORMATION IN PRACTICE: UNLOCKING A DILEMMA

Control was an issue in Kerry's mothering. She could not tolerate the way her daughter Samantha was pulling away and would refer to her own mother's strict and effective parenting as she set confining limits and gave little space for her daughter to express her own burgeoning identity. Things got tense when her daughter, feeling too cramped under this strict, non-empathetic regime, started to act out, first in small ways—such as by not letting her mom know where she was—and then in larger ways—by taking illegal substances.

Samantha felt misunderstood. She told me that no matter what she said or did, her mom wouldn't listen. This wasn't far from the truth. Over the course of our sessions, her mother's dilemma emerged: She had a brother who had died of a drug overdose. She felt her parents' response had been too slack, and she swore that she would never be one of those parents who were "friends" with their kids. But by going overboard in her desire to not repeat what she saw as her parents' mistake, she was inhabiting the polar opposite.

The internal dilemma for Kerry was that she wanted to connect with her daughter, but her unprocessed grief about her brother wouldn't allow that closeness. Though she recognized she was being too strict, her fear that she would lose her daughter in the same way she lost her brother kept her from examining the underlying causes.

Once we unwound the dilemma and invited in all the feelings of grief, fear of attachment, and subsequent disappointment (if she connected more deeply with her daughter and then lost her), Kerry was able to come to a more moderate stance as it related to Samantha's curfews and daily life.

EXERCISE: RESOLVING DILEMMAS

What dilemma—as it pertains to your teen—are you harboring? What do you find goes around and around in your own mind about how to be with your teen? If you can pause, and go a bit more deeply, are you able to *feel* where the dilemma originates? Is it in your heart? Your belly? What issue and set of feelings are you truly grappling with that are taking the form of this unanswerable question?

TRANSFORMATION IN PRACTICE:
THE PARADOX OF INACTION

Violet was an anxious mom, and June was an anxious daughter. Violet was worried about June, who was nineteen and in her first year of college. "I wish I could figure out what to say to make it better for her," she told me many times.

Interestingly, neither mother nor daughter was aware of her own anxiety because it manifested in storms of action and ever-shifting symptoms, such as workaholism, eating disorders, and paralysis around decision making.

Mental illnesses like anxiety and depression are truly like monsters with their own anatomy and survival mechanisms. One of anxiety's most successful survival tools is playing unconscious "tag" with the people it infects. I'm sure you've noticed that when you're in a room with someone who is palpably anxious, but who is reassuring you that he is "totally fine"—even while his brow is perspiring, his eyes are darting about, and he is clearly anything *but* fine—you start to feel anxious yourself. "You're it," says the anxiety monster. And on it goes.

This was the case with Violet and June. Often it happens that a parent's and teen's core wounds rub against each other, creating a collective wound that is deeper than each might have individually. It was through my thorough work with each of them separately—a separation that was difficult for both of them—that each could finally shed the patterns of anxiety and rest in a deeper calm. June had to accept a deeper longing for her mother than she ever felt capable of acknowledging. Both mother and daughter suffered from a common ailment, which is attempting to solve emotional pain through action.

While action can be part of the formula for healing, the main action required is actually *inaction*. Inaction involves acceptance, grief, and the expanded capacity to tolerate one's own and the other person's realities no matter how messy or threatening they may seem. I worked with both women's inner children and asked the powerful question that is often at the heart of the matter in many symptoms of emotional disease: "Where are you on the self-love scale?"

Violet answered, "Do you mean do I love myself? I don't know—I have faults." Body image and eating issues started young for her and were nonverbally transmitted to her daughter through a hyper-awareness of healthy food and counting calories. June inherited the same problems through simply watching her mom as she grew up. Both mother and daughter struggled with high levels of self-criticism and needed inner child work and energetic healing in addition to limbic reregulation in order to heal. It was ultimately rewarding work for all involved.

After our work, both Violet and June reported that for the first time in their lives, they didn't feel the "anxiety monster" dominating their communication and plunging them into downward spirals of disconnection and disappointment. Once the monster was quelled, each woman could be present for the other with her authentic self.

So now Violet doesn't try to figure out what she can say to make it better for her daughter; she knows and accepts that there is actually nothing more to say. But there is a way to *be* that provides infinite comfort for both of them and promotes bonding with her daughter. This connection is as invisible yet as powerful as cosmic radiation. It is a connection that we all understand deep in our bones, a connection for which there are no words.

EXERCISE: CULTIVATING COMPASSION FOR SELF

Perhaps the most important step you can take to enlarge the lens of your relationship with your teen is to cultivate compassion for yourself. If this feels uncomfortable to you, for the sake of your teen I urge you not to shrug it off.

Lack of self-love is at the core of many disorders, and much of the time patients are so distracted by symptoms that they don't even know they lack self-love, or that it is an essential building block of psychological health. Getting to this awareness is a process and a necessary step in building the self-love at the basis of healthy relationships with ourselves and others. That's why I'm closing this chapter with an exercise that is as much a meditation as it is a prayer.

> Find a comfortable place to sit. Breathe. Think of someone you know who cares about you deeply. Imagine this person. Maybe it's your grandmother, maybe it's a friend, or maybe it's a spiritually inspiring figure like Jesus or the Buddha. Maybe it's your dog. It doesn't matter, so long as this person or being has unconditional positive regard* for you. Notice the sadness or mourning that might emerge as you open yourself to the trickle of compassion from another.
>
> Feel this being touch you lovingly or smile or just *be* with you as you open to this sweet energy of love. You are

---

*My thanks to Carl Rogers for the phrase "unconditional positive regard."

perfect just as you are. You are perfect because you are who you are.

As you begin to feel the outpouring from this being, place your hand on your heart to intensify the feeling and to ignite your compassionate self. Then ask all the cells of your body to be imprinted with this sense of love and compassion for you as you are. Perfection.

Now let's flex this muscle of compassion as you receive it and send it out to someone who is suffering. You are now radiating compassion, soft waves rippling out. You are now embodying compassion. You are wishing that no beings will have to suffer, ever.

And now, again, turn that compassionate energy toward yourself. Feel how life is hard for you. And wish for yourself that you will not suffer. Radiate compassion toward yourself and the stresses that you experience.

Invite this prayer: *May I find peace when my teen tells me something stressful.* Sense the compassion flowing through you. Feel yourself radiating it outward.

3

TRANSFORMATIVE STRATEGY #3:
DON'T GRASP—LET GO

Your children are not your children,
They are the sons and daughters of Life's longing for itself.
They come through you but not from you,
And though they are with you, yet they belong not to you.

—Kahlil Gibran

THE WRITER ANNE LAMOTT POETICALLY DESCRIBES being a parent as having a "heart that runs around outside our body."[*] So I am never surprised at the helpless, breathless calls I receive from parents who are wishing to find solutions to their teen's problems, even though they know somewhere deep inside that it is now their job to begin to

---

[*]Anne Lamott, *Operating Instructions: A Journal of My Son's First Year* (New York: Anchor Books, 1993).

relinquish control so as to truly support the safety and success of their teen's transition into adulthood.

Sometimes the situation with your teen feels out of control because it is—out of *your* control, that is! In her seminal work on adolescents,[*] Dr. Lynn Ponton powerfully describes what she terms "risk-taking" behaviors as a necessary part of a teen's normal, healthy developmental striving. While many parents intellectually know this to be true, they are emotionally unable to avoid being drawn into a power struggle. It's not easy. "I'm the family doormat," "No teen is going to disrespect me like that," and "We don't do *that* in our family" are just some of the parental protestations I hear. Because parents are unable to acknowledge what they are really feeling and to entertain the paradox of being firm yet letting go, when they are triggered by their teen's risk-taking behaviors, these well-meaning moms and dads are ineffective at both maintaining the relationship they desire and communicating the values they hold dear. This chapter is about the paradox of letting go while holding on. It's about understanding what you are really feeling and how to effectively react when your teen flips you the bird and screeches out of the driveway in your car. This chapter will illuminate how you untangle yourself from the confusing power struggles and exasperating breaches of trust your teen demonstrates so that you can maintain firm boundaries, communicate your values, and maintain a close relationship with your teen.

---

[*]Lynn Ponton, *The Romance of Risk: Why Teenagers Do the Things They Do* (New York: Basic Books, 1987).

ENTERTAINING PARADOX?
THAT SOUNDS COMPLICATED

Peter Blos,[*] one of the first child psychoanalysts and a pioneer in adolescent psychology, offered a deep and unique understanding of the teenage struggle. He laid down the reasons for the complexity parents face with their teens. In his description of the developmental stage teens are in, he pointed to a second individuation process, one that is parallel to the stage that children go through at around age two. During this early period, as you may recall, your toddler is tentatively exploring the world and then returning to your arms, sometimes filled with pride and sometimes in tears. Anyone who is around teens will recognize this pattern: One day they are a young adult who wants nothing to do with you and knows it all; the next they are holding your hand in the mall. Paradox! As author Michael Simon puts it, "Teens want to know you are still available to them, that they are trusted and can begin to trust their own judgment. They want to know that things are in their control, that they have choices and can get over the fear that they have that they won't be able to do the right thing."[†]

Is it any wonder that the emotional engagements they initiate have parallels to those of toddlers? Your ability as a parent to hold two opposites—"I see the cranky child in the angry teen; I see the budding adult in the wailing baby"—will

---

[*]Peter Blos, *On Adolescence* (Glencoe, IL: Free Press of Glencoe, 1962).

[†]Michael Y. Simon, *The Approximate Parent: Discovering the Strategies That Work with Your Teenager* (Oakland, CA: Fine Optics, 2012), 224.

serve your ability to have empathy and communicate effectively with your adolescent.

MAKING SPACE AS LETTING GO: THE CASE OF ANNA

Anna was a Mexican American seventeen-year-old who came to me at the request of her high school counselor. She was an excellent student, was considered an "overachiever" by peers and teachers, but recently had started missing classes, and her parents were concerned that she seemed depressed. Like many first-generation children of immigrants, Anna was not alone in feeling more pressures to succeed than other teens. Both her parents had been born in Mexico, and Anna had been given a lot of responsibility to navigate the logistics of her and her family's life ever since she was a young child. Now, as a teen, she was the subject of extremely high expectations from her loving and hardworking parents.

My question was this: What was Anna acting out that her parents were not aware of? What did she need to embody that was being communicated unconsciously in this family? And what was the paradox that these parents needed to learn to accept?

Anna's dad was a successful contractor, and her mom had her own in-home day care. They were understandably concerned that if Anna continued to miss classes and exhibit signs of depression during her important junior year, she would forfeit her opportunities to get into a good college. As neither parent had attended college, this was an important milestone that they saw as nonnegotiable.

When I met with Anna, her anxiety about succeeding "for her parents" and also finding her own way, independent of her parents' expectations, was palpable. She did not know how to find her own path without rejecting the pressures that her parents were lovingly, but also unconsciously, imposing. My work with the parents involved supporting them to trust their daughter and to notice the fears that may have come from their own challenging journey to make it in this country, rather than focusing on Anna's potential failure. My work with Anna was to support her to find other, less self-sabotaging ways to clear space for her experimentation besides rejecting school. In a meeting with Anna and her parents, we worked on their ability to express their fears openly and to then allow Anna the space to find her own way.

I often ask parents to think about how they can honor their dreams for their children while also allowing their children to have their own journeys. I encourage parents to ask themselves, What vision of my child am I holding that may not be aligned with my child's vision of herself?

TEEN TIP 101: LET'S TALK ABOUT TRUST

Trust: the glue that binds intimate relationships. Trust is what teens strive for and deeply desire from those around them, especially parents. I call it the currency of adolescence because it is necessary for all exchanges and it can be bartered, negotiated, lost, and then refound. It's the badge of adulthood. It's also the very thing teens tamper with in their escapades with friends, when pushing the limits with school, and in their other freedom-seeking behaviors.

In my practice I find that parents' ability to trust their teen can become eroded in power struggles that test the bond of connection. Once this happens, communication breaks down, and the relationship is in trouble. This is problematic not just because it is painful for parents to be lied to by their teen and to have their trust betrayed. Research tells us that the most important factor in ensuring that parents and their children emerge from the teen years with an intact and healthy relationship is their trust in each other.

"How am I supposed to trust him when he lies, pushes every boundary, and abuses all the freedoms I allow?" a parent will exclaim in my office. "How do I teach ethical behavior and promote accountability when she curses, is rude, and won't let me in on anything that's going on?" says another parent in crisis. "Honesty is one of the most important lessons I want to impart. I will not tolerate deception," a hurt and angry dad asserts. Of course, these parents' goals are worthy and valid. But how to achieve them without the power struggle?

Most parents are triggered—their conscious or unconscious fears set into action—when teens challenge their trust. "I didn't mean to get that drunk and end up in the ER, I swear." When your trust is broken, it is natural to react. "She stayed in the park and didn't call, and now I'm disappointed and feel betrayed." Your teen's rites of passage will challenge boundaries and expectations. How you navigate this choppy sea requires a nuanced and somewhat contradictory principle. If we don't trust someone, it is impossible to cultivate positive emotions of connection and love. And yet testing their parents' trust is one way teens express their desire for separation and distance. When you take it literally, as a betrayal of trust, you may miss what your teen is telling you. Seeing your teen as the adult he wishes to be, even if you don't fully treat him with all the freedoms afforded an adult, is a first step in seeing your teen as separate from you. This step, while seemingly simple, may bring up challenges, including unbearable loss for some parents. For other parents, acknowledging their teens' budding adulthood triggers control issues or unresolved grief. When the bonds of connection have been appropriately nurtured between parent and teen from early childhood, the relationship can weather the storms that test trust.

THE PARADOX OF TRUST: IT'S NOT ALWAYS THE WAY IT SEEMS

Your teen might want your trust, but their sometimes erratic and irresponsible actions can result in an inability to let them out of your sight. The solution: Show them how to separate from you and explore on their own. And then let go of your expectations.

Teens learn from what you do, not from what you say. As you micromanage their college process, their sports career, or their moral evolution, are you demonstrating fear or trust? Instead of fears ruling our actions in any given moment, can you practice the calm belief in your teen's capacity? Trust is what young people need in order to grow and thrive.

The art of taking charge while surrendering becomes essential when parenting adolescents. You are called to set limits to their ever-expanding need for freedom while acknowledging that they are in fact becoming young adults. This is why the ability to tolerate paradox and ambiguity becomes an essential skill for parenting teens.

As one teen put it, "I know I look like your typical train wreck of a teen. I landed myself in the emergency room the first time I drank. But now I know my limits—myself! I can't learn this from what my parents *tell* me. My parents are afraid I'm going to become a homeless prostitute just because I don't fit into their perfect box and act like them! I'm so different from them."

The paradox here: This teen's experience-rich approach to life (she prefers parties to studying but still maintains reasonable grades) may not give her the life her parents believe she should live. But maybe she's not like them, and maybe that's okay. Perhaps you think you are accepting your teen as she is, but somewhere deep inside, a place that is obvious to your teen but hidden to yourself, there are judgments, fears, negative narratives of doom, or subtle messages of disapproval.

The inner trajectory you construct for your teen may not have anything to do with their lived realities—which are flexible and changing. Some teens learn through experience rather than in a school setting. Some teens have no interest in having a lot of friends, playing sports, or dressing the way their parents think they should. This can be upsetting to parents who have a rigid definition of success.

Many of the teens I see in my practice are more comfortable learning in real-life situations than in the classroom. The thirteen- and fourteen-year-olds are distracted with philosophical, existential questions: "What is the point of all of this? What is my purpose?" Parents who invalidate these concerns and urge their teens to simply focus on school and get on with it will lose their children's trust, and their teens will persist with these questions through less desirable experiments with substance use and other types of delinquent behavior. Our school system favors the teen who learns in a particular way: the student who is comfortable learning in a classroom and following a teacher's instructions rather than learning through experience. So teens with deep questions or alternative beliefs or behaviors can often feel marginalized and alienated.

Unfortunately, there aren't a lot of outlets for teens to test their limits, their knowledge, and their experience in ways that are developmentally appropriate. Teens have a specific set of tasks that are their developmental rites. Madeline Levine in *The Price of Privilege* explains that teens are developing a sense of self. So, according to Levine, parents want their teens to learn how to:

- be effective in the world
- have a sense that they are in control of their lives
- form deep and enduring relationships
- value and accept themselves
- have hobbies
- know how to take care of themselves

A teen is developing at a rapid rate, and this can cause emotional instability. When we understand the details we can make room for the birth of this new self.

MANAGING YOUR OWN DISCOMFORT

Trial and error, experience through their bodies, and adventure and risk are the ways that teens naturally learn. I have one teen in my practice who is "packed for Paris" under her bed. Her father takes this as a sign that she is not grounded in reality and deserves less freedom and privilege than she so sorely seeks. By understanding the psychological reasons for her living through this dream, her dad can be more compassionate and connected while negotiating her freedoms realistically.

Rather than offering your teen formulaic solutions, move to the outer reaches of your own comfort and of your own imagination to create a solution. Try to empathize with the feeling behind the request. For example, I had a fourteen-year-old who wanted to quit school to work full-time at a homeless shelter in order to give her life meaning. Of course, quitting school may not have been the best answer, but she was not well served by her parents' dismissive response. Her search for a deeper reason for her being was developmentally appropriate and could have been an opening for a dialogue with her parents about how to reduce her academic stress and reevaluate her activities to include engaging meaningfully with the world around her—for example, through service.

KNOW YOUR TRIGGERS

Take a moment to reflect: While you may champion your child to those around you, is there a characteristic or set of behaviors that you reject in your teen? Even just slightly? If so, where does it come from? Is this belief, even if never expressed, helping your teen? What would calm this fear or transform this belief?

Parents all get triggered by different aspects of their teen. Revisiting your Trigger Map (from Chapter 1) and going deeper here is worthwhile as you work to let go. Finding out your particular pattern of triggers, becoming aware of them, and then moving toward a place of calm in the face of the triggers will help you ride the waves of your teen's challenges and maintain your trust in them. One mother, a lawyer for whom control was a big trigger, had a difficult time when her teen demonstrated what I would call "appropriate" levels of deception. That sounds strange—being honest is the cornerstone of all relationships, right? Well, yes and no.

Teens use minor, not harmful, moments of deception to create distance and their own space as a developmentally appropriate movement away from parents. For example, maybe your son is not at the mall; he's at Lawrence's house for the afternoon. Unless you're concerned that your teen is engaging in harmful or dangerous behavior, tolerating these little white lies is part of riding the wave of your teen's separation initiative. The lawyer mom, for whom control and honesty were very important and almost rigidly maintained, entered the trust-mistrust downward spiral with her teen after her daughter lied about where she had been. This resulted in the mom grounding her daughter, the daughter feeling misunderstood and criticized and becoming more rebellious, and the relationship moving to a stagnant place where the communication degraded while the daughter was engaging in increasingly dangerous activities.

My work with one mom, Elowan, involved having her revisit memories of her own childhood. She was the daughter of a mother who had suffered trauma growing up in an economically and emotionally impoverished environment, so she had to be in control of all around her or her world would fall apart—or so she thought. She maintained that same ironclad hold on all around her until her daughter came to teach her a lesson about that. As I invited Elowan to feel the feelings of being out of control, and to surrender to some of the unknown aspects of her daughter's life, she was able to communicate more honestly with her daughter. As she developed less rigid expectations, her daughter was more willing to make compromises, and their relationship slowly improved.

KNOW YOUR HOPES AND FEARS

In my experience, these are some of the most common triggers parents have. Do any of these sound familiar?

- Fear of my teen becoming independent
- Fear of not being in control
- Fear of loss

- Fear of chaos
- Fear of my teen's substance use
- Fear about my teen's future prospects
- Fear that my teen is nothing like me
- Fear that my teen is too much like me

I have found that the first step toward learning how to let go while also guiding and staying connected to your teen is to know your fears. Usually there is one worry around which most of our worries cluster. For some it's about their children's health. For others it's about success, popularity, or other concerns. Take a moment to dive deep into that place that may stay mostly undercover. Before you move on, I want you to narrow it down to just one concern by filling in the blank: "The number one worry I have about my child is _____."

Connect to the Emotion Behind the Emotion

Now try to answer this question: What's the emotion behind your number one fear?

Most fears are connected to some aspect of mourning that has yet to be done. Maybe you have sacrificed a lot for your child, and you need to mourn the loss of those years of making friends or doing other things before you can let go. Maybe letting go elicits an existential sense of loss you've never faced. We're all mortal, but some of us live as if we will live forever, never facing the inevitability of our death until our child invites us to notice it when they leave the house. All things begin and end. It's a tough one to accept!

A common scenario I see in my practice is parents who are treating their fifteen-year-olds like nine-year-olds. "She doesn't want to do anything with me anymore," one mother laments. Or, "I have nothing to say to her. When I give her advice that she used to love getting, now she walks away or rolls her eyes." Parents will find themselves rejected when they fail to see that their teen naturally wishes to be alone, to choose their friends over their parents, and to be treated as the expert on their own life.

The ability to know loneliness—at a deep level to accept loss and to bear separation—is fundamental to all of the strategies we have reviewed so far. It is a paradox: as a parent you must stay connected emotionally to continue to shepherd your teen into the next chapter of their life, but staying connected emotionally requires a large dose of tolerating separation between your teen and yourself *and* grieving and the losses within yourself. So staying connected to your teen might not look or feel like staying connected as your teen starts to distance herself, gives you mixed signals about being with you, and pushes your buttons. Through her own pain she reminds you of your own demons. So, to truly, authentically stay connected to your child you must create space, between the two of you and within yourself. There are many corridors you must travel in order to stay close to your child in the way that they need you to be.

It is painful and uncomfortable when your teen doesn't want to talk to you or isn't who you imagined he would become. This triggers self-judgment: *I am a bad parent.* When you learn to accept and embrace painful feelings, then true transformation can occur. Pain comes in all varieties: the pain of separation, the tears of losing control, the tugs at the heart as you see your teen suffer. As you develop tools to move toward and feel these emotions, the path to clarity and effective problem solving will emerge.

TRANSFORMATION IN PRACTICE: CARLOS AND SUSAN

Carlos was the child of a depressed mother and a driven, perfectionistic father. Chaos reigned in his home after his parents divorced and he was left to be raised by his mom, who filled her days with variations on the cocktail party. As Carlos described it, "No one was home," even though the house with filled with chaotic adults indulging in alcoholic partying. Carlos's life was built around avoiding disorder, internal and external, at all costs.

Enter his daughter, Susan, age thirteen. After she was put on academic probation and found drinking in her room with her friends, Carlos was ready to send Susan away. "I will not deal with chaos," he said, fighting back tears. "I cannot accept this." Carlos was also dismayed that Susan was hanging around with the "wrong crowd" and wondered how he might put restrictions on Susan's choices of friends. Carlos demonstrated the moral perfectionism and rigidity common to many adult children of alcoholics: "Honesty is the pillar around which I built my life. Other parents might be okay with lies, but not this dad. I will not partake in the moral decay I see around me." Carlos was determined to mold Susan in the image he saw as fit and, more importantly, safe.

Parents are understandably wired to be triggered by things that affect the safety of their children. Lying pushes against that safety concern in a deep way. Susan was part of a group of teens we might call precocious, but who were mostly reasonable and not engaging in extremely risky behaviors. Most parents expect teens age thirteen or fourteen to ease into adolescence with less risky behaviors because their actions are more restricted than those of their older counterparts (who may be driving, going to the mall, staying out late at night). But it is precisely *because* they are so restricted that they often push the envelope with more adventurous behaviors as attempts to gain the freedoms they crave. This is important because fathers like Carlos often fear that if their teen is procuring alcohol, lying, and having problems at school at age thirteen, then what's in store at seventeen? But with the freedoms that come with later teen years, such as extended curfews, these teens often find a more responsible stride.

Carlos and Susan found themselves stuck in the trust-mistrust cycle, and it was driving a wedge into their close relationship. This was devastating to Carlos, who had given up a more lucrative and demanding career track to invest his emotional energy into his children. He considered his relationships with them his life's work, which made his grip on his vision of this relationship even more tenacious and inflexible.

Understanding the Trust-Mistrust Cycle

The first order of business was to meet with Carlos and Susan together to understand the communication breakdown. Each party was asked to sacrifice something that felt important for the sake of a gain that each wanted. Carlos was asked to examine his vision of the perfect teenager in order to listen to Susan's version of why she had lied. I proposed that Carlos's repaired ability to communicate with Susan would be more satisfying than maintaining his vision of the "perfect teen." He reluctantly agreed.

Susan was invited to understand her father's fears about her safety and to do her best to reduce those through accountability behaviors such as more communication and less lying. In exchange for Susan's "sacrifice," she would be trusted more and given more freedom. Sometimes this kind of work takes a single session; sometimes it takes months or longer. The duration depends on the quality of the bond and the flexibility of each teen and parent.

KNOW YOUR PROJECTIONS

What fears, conceptions, expectations, or challenging beliefs do you bring from your own experience of being a teenager? How were you parented as a teen? Are there images of what a teen should or shouldn't do that are rooted in your own experiences and not actually part of your own teen's experience? Were you a wild teen, so you fear your daughter will be the same? A repressed teen whose unexpressed inner teen is afraid of what terrors lurk in these years? If you have anxiety, then when your teen texts you that she had a few drinks at a party and asks for a ride—actually demonstrating somewhat responsible behavior—do you leap to "My teen is a drug abuser"? If you have depression, do you fear your teen's grouchy, isolating behaviors will bring him to dark places from which he will never emerge?

Spend some time reflecting on your own experiences as a teen, your assumptions, and some of the free-floating emotions that are *yours* and only yours. You'll need to recognize your own projections—emotions, usually unconscious, that you're attributing to your teen that are really coming from inside you. This will keep the communication cleaner and more effective between you and your adolescent.

INVITING THE HIGHER SELF

The term "Higher Self" is shorthand for a wise, all-knowing aspect of ourselves. The Higher Self acts from love rather than from fear and seeks communion with the world rather than division or any other emotion that could be destructive like petty self-interest or anger. We know intuitively when we are acting from our Higher Selves; some may know it as the divine aspect of the self. I believe that just as you have a Higher Self or Spirit that is larger than your logical mind can know, your teen has one too. Even the least woo-woo teens and parents I have worked with produce great insights when I invite them to access this aspect of themselves.

This concept has been codified in traditional psychology by Marsha Linehan, the founder of dialectical behavior therapy. She uses the term "Wise Mind" to describe the experience of integrating the rational mind with the emotional mind and intuition.[*]

Jasmine, age seventeen, called herself the black sheep of her family; she said the members of her family "lived in a square box and liked it." She threatened to run away and had burned many bridges through risk-taking behaviors. However, her Higher Self was wise. She knew that she didn't want to live the buttoned-up, stressed-out lives her parents lived, and she needed to test some waters to find out who she was.

Seth, an eighteen-year-old with depression who had lost his mother to suicide when he was a baby, had a deep and fruitful relationship with his Higher Self. While enduring the strain of living with a challenging stepmother, the indignities of high school social drama, and the pain of an absent father, he took solace in messages he would receive while meditating with his Higher Self. These included compassion for his stepmother, the ability to have distance from the meaningless social drama, and investment in other relationships with males in his family and outside of it who provided him with the support he so longed for in a father. It's amazing the wisdom and mature insights these higher beings have!

Parents ask me, "How can I encourage my teen to be in touch with this Higher Self?" My answer is, like the Buddha

---

[*]Marsha Linehan, *DBT Skills Training Manual*, 2nd ed. (New York: Guilford, 2015).

urges, "Be the change you wish to see." Meditate, get good therapy, and find processes to develop your self-awareness and your own self-actualization. Grow your own joy and peace, and you will contact the best in you, engendering the best in your teen—most of the time! When your mood, actions, and reactions with your child are motivated from an expansive, loving place, your teen, unless burdened by other serious problems, will naturally find their way to communicating with these higher aspects of themselves. Teens aren't particularly interested in their parent as guru or spiritual teacher, so attempts to explain a step-by-step process to the Higher Self after dinner will be met with resistance at best. Instead, spend a few moments each day imagining what your own Higher Self looks like and what its message to you is. This will create an invisible yet palpable experience for you that will positively influence your teen.

EXERCISE: INVITING TRUST

Now that we've reviewed the importance of trusting your teen (no matter what), cleared the projections, and demonstrated that teens too can be wise, let's work on our own relationship to Trust. Just as I believe that "self" describes our more fear-driven, ego self, while "Self" describes our love-driven Spirit self, so too do I believe that there is a distinction between "trust" and "Trust."

Teens will most definitely challenge their parents' trust. They will seek freedom and the experiences they need to grow. If they lie, sometimes it's to create their own narrative.

We can judge it as good or bad, but it is likely to occur. I find that by moving from trust to Trust, we can endure the small challenges to the trust that binds and infuse the relationship with Spirit that sustains. What am I talking about?

Using the other transformative strategies like enduring emotions and enlarging the lens, you can take your relationship growth one step further. When your teen lies, finds himself in a deep mess, continues to challenge your deepest values, or is skating on the edge of disaster, you look for the Trust. Ask yourself these questions when inviting in the Trust:

- What is my teen's Higher Self trying to accomplish? Is there a value to his growth in this behavior that, if I understood and validated it, might disappear?
- Where is my ego entering this power struggle? Where are old beliefs about how things "should be" preventing me from seeing how things are and moving to acceptance?
- When I'm interacting with my teen, am I in myself or in my Self? Am I defensive, reactive, aggressive, critical, fear-driven? Or do I seek to understand rather than to be understood?
- When I move to give a consequence for my teen's egregious behavior, am I coming from a place of calm conviction that a consequence would serve as an important communication or boundary for my teen's actions? Or am I feeling angry, spiteful, and desperate to act in order to exert control?
- How susceptible am I to the "shoulds" of parenting teens as opposed to being tuned in to the unique ways I know

my child best lives in the world? Do I become enraged when my teen drops an f-bomb after a long day, no food, and an argument where I've denied her a freedom? Or do I quietly endure what I feel is a rude behavior and discuss my expectations for her manners and etiquette at a time when we are both calm and reasonable?

Yes, that's me—just like Mother Teresa, you might be thinking! I never said this would be easy. But acting and reacting out of fear and mistrust create consequences that aren't easy to face either. And, as we know from quantum physics, particles that vibrate at a certain frequency attract other particles that vibrate at the same frequency. Trust attracts Trust, in other words.

FINDING YOUR PATTERN OF HOLDING ON

Lisa, mother of seventeen-year-old Evan, drew the line at tattoos. When Evan got a large image of his dog, face in a menacing growl, across his shoulder, Lisa felt betrayed and tempted to disown him. As the daughter of Holocaust survivors who were tattooed as part of the extermination process, Lisa was deeply repulsed by tattoos and felt that her loyalty to her ancestors would be betrayed if she changed her position. So the meaning of Evan's tattoo for Lisa was one of deep betrayal and even aggression. "How could he make such a statement against our entire family and especially his grandparents, who escaped from years of oppression and almost death. Doesn't he get it?"

For Evan, the tattoo stood for his deep bond with his dog, something he hoped would support him as he ventured out to live on his own after high school. Rather than being able to see her son's tattoo as his own expression of separation and identity, Lisa's relationship to her family's past was keeping her from being able to step back and let go appropriately. This led to months of no communication between the two, which resulted in a visit to see me. To be clear, I was not counseling Lisa to "accept the tattoo." Parents set the moral and behavioral directives. Instead, I offer tips so that parents can actually be more influential with their teen because they're able to remain in relationship and in communication through these conflicts.

Letting go is one of the most difficult aspects of parenting, but it's also part of the job description. It isn't easy, and it requires a profound knowledge of oneself. It's good and natural to have a deep attachment to your teen. Continuing that healthy attachment, in fact, gives your teen the best chance at success. However, you also need to allow your teen the space to become themselves. They need room to express ideas that you may find reprehensible, to be with people you might not like, and to engage in behaviors you may fear or despise. How do you give them room to do this? First, by knowing how you create space and let go in other areas of your life.

EXERCISE: LETTING GO

Answer this series of questions to understand what's holding you back from letting go:

- What is easy for you to let go of? Name a few simple events or moments during which you have let go.
- What is difficult for you to let go of? Name a few times it was difficult to let go.
- Have there been traumatic events in your life with your child that have made it more difficult to make space? (If so, you might want to consider therapy to work on healing from them.)
- What was your life like as a teen? How did the separation from your own parents go? Was it abrupt? Smooth? Did they stay connected as you rebelled? Or did you never rebel but always played the role of the good girl or boy?
- Are there traumatic separations or losses in your family of origin that may be unconsciously affecting your ability to tolerate separation or loss?

DIFFICULT WATERS: TEENS AND TECHNOLOGY

Teens today have to deal with something that their parents did not: the encroaching role of technology in every aspect of their lives, particularly their social lives. Teens are outwardly focused and are concerned about what others think of them. In fact, they use these impressions as their primary input for identity formation. Parents, nevertheless, wish their teens could think for themselves and not care so much about their friends' opinions. They are surprised by the extent of their teen's outward focus and believe it is volitional. My invitation to parents is to consider that it is not. Can you change a zebra's stripes? Like it or not, where they stand in relation to their peers is of central importance, informing almost every decision an adolescent makes.[*]

Of course, the internet has complicated this phenomenon. In the "networked publics of the lives of teens," writer Danah Boyd points out, there are qualities of "persistence, searchability, exact copyability, and invisible audiences. These properties fundamentally alter social dynamics complicating the ways in which people interact."[†] Michael Simon, in *The Approximate Parent*, adds: "Since data is always available 24/7, flexibly represented, easy to manipulate and falsify, fast and easy to distribute, hard to get rid of and often created and consumed with many, many others at the same time, the chances for hurt feelings, misunderstandings, embarrassment, pain and heartache increase, making the Internet a good place for a teen to feel bad."[‡]

Much more has and will be written on this topic as we come to terms with the evolving impact of technology on all of our lives, but suffice it to say that letting go becomes even more challenging and complex when your teen needs to Instagram into the night or can't be separated from his laptop because he needs it for school assignments. Of course, age-appropriate protections and limits should accompany

---

[*]Simon, *The Approximate Parent*, 177.

[†]Danah Boyd, *Why Youth Love Social Network Sites: The Role of Networked Publics in Teenage Social Life* (Cambridge, MA: MIT Press, 2007), 2.

[‡]Simon, *The Approximate Parent*, 176.

internet privileges—all of which leads to more negotiation. While I find that it is technically more difficult to guide parents to let go in the digital age, the principles remain the same, and so does the eternal question: How do I trust my teen, give them room to experiment, offer them guidelines, and then let them find their own voice?

4

TRANSFORMATIVE STRATEGY #4:
DISCOVER PROFOUND PURPOSE

He who has a why to live for can bear almost any how.

—Friedrich Nietzsche[*]

Y OU AND YOUR TEEN HAVE A SPECIFIC REASON FOR
being in each other's lives. The challenges and the
rewards of this relationship are buried deep inside you.
Being emotionally connected to your teen is essential to
discovering this purpose. Psychologists describe this kind
of connection as "attached" and have built whole theories
around this most primal of bonds. Another way to describe
this important quality of the relationship parents have with

---

[*]Quoted in Viktor E. Frankl, *Man's Search for Meaning* (Boston: Beacon,
1959).

their children is to "limbically know" them.* Children with healthy attachments are much better able to cope with life's stressors and much better able to evolve into healthy, resilient teenagers.

What is the behavior of a parent who limbically knows their teen, who is attached? In his book *Brainstorm*, psychiatrist Dan Siegel describes a skill called "mindsight," which captures what parents who wish to have a healthy attachment relationship to their children do:

> Mindsight is the ability to truly "see" or know the mind. Seeing the mind, being empathic, compassionate and kind. Mindsight includes three fundamental skills: 1) Insight, the ability to sense your own inner mental life. 2) Empathy, the ability to sense the inner mental life of another person. 3) Integration, the ability to link different parts of something into an interconnected whole.†

Developmental psychologist Gordon Neufeld describes other ways parents can connect to their teens. He writes that "greetings should collect the eyes, a smile, a nod. Other ways to attach include 1) affection 2) a twinkle in your eye 3) being on your child's 'side.'" Finally, Neufeld comments on something that I have seen to be true: "The will to connect must

---

*Thomas Lewis, Fari Amini, and Richard Lannon, *A General Theory of Love* (New York: Vintage Books, 2000).
†Daniel J. Siegel, *Brainstorm: The Power and Purpose of the Teenage Brain* (New York: Tarcher/Penguin, 2013), 39–40.

be in the parent before there is anything positive for the child to respond to."*

It might seem that all parents have this will. Nevertheless, the will must be accompanied by a certain competence to connect and a consistency to do it over time. A parent's past wounds can interrupt this necessary, consistent capacity to form healthy attachments with their child. Once their child reaches the teen years, if this attachment is not well established it will be nearly impossible to connect, to positively influence their behaviors, and to continue to relate to them as they begin to separate.

The centrality of connection in human relations is even implicated as a central factor in substance use. Author Johann Hari cites research suggesting that addiction is a result of human disconnection, not just brain chemistry. "If we can't connect with each other, we will connect with anything we find—the whirr of a roulette wheel or the prick of a syringe." Hari cites professor Peter Cohen, who says, "We should stop talking about 'addiction' altogether, and instead call it 'bonding.' A heroin addict has bonded with heroin because she couldn't bond as fully with anything else." Hari goes on to say that "the opposite of addiction is not sobriety. It is human connection."†

So finding your purpose in your teen's challenges requires that you are connected to yourself *and* connected to

---

*Gordon Neufeld and Gabor Mate, *Hold onto Your Kids: Why Parents Need to Matter More Than Peers* (New York: Ballantine Books, 2006), 182, 219.
†Johann Hari, "The Likely Cause of Addiction Has Been Discovered, and It Is Not What You Think," *Huffington Post*, January 20, 2015.

your teen. In his challenges and his gifts, your child provides glimpses that can point you in the direction of your true purpose. It may not always be what you want, but I believe it's always what you ultimately need. Your teen shares some of your strengths and vulnerabilities; where they are stumbling can be a clue to where you may also need to heal. The overly controlling mother, after suffering through innumerable challenges with her teen (including a trip to rehab), heals her own core feelings of inadequacy, which have held her back in life. Through this healing, a deepened appreciation of her life results. The lessons you learn from seeing your teen's problems in this light are varied and profound. Massive internal shifts can happen, new careers can take shape, and chronic anxiety can yield to simple moments of ease. I've seen it happen.

As one mother told me, "My daughter's challenges to me about my mothering are like lancing the wound that opened up my shame, my sense of regret, so that I could finally have the space to find out who I was without the masks." This statement came after many sessions of intense, contentious shouting matches between this woman and her thirteen-year-old daughter, during which the daughter would bitterly criticize her mother for everything she did, and the mother would put her arm out with her hand in the "stop" position, face bright red, and shout back in defense. Each session was a small dose of medicine for the mother, as she realized that her daughter was indeed her teacher and would be the person to force her to take down her defenses and face her wounds so she could finally find her purpose.

In finding the profound purpose you are meant to pursue through your teen, I invite you to discover your deepest meaning in life and to approach your parenting in new ways. Your teen is your map. Instead of arguing, find the pause. Instead of fearing, find the faith. Instead of fixating on how your teen is doomed, open to the truth of her unlimited potential. Instead of reacting like the mother of this thirteen-year-old, who spent months resisting and avoiding her daughter, open yourself to the painful lessons she wishes to teach you by looking in the mirror. Attune not only to the macro aspects of your lives—friends, life after high school, the future—but also to the subatomic, wispy elements: those mysterious ways you and your teen feel and think that truly determine the flow of your lives together.

EXERCISE: UNTANGLING THE MATRIX

Find a quiet place, and close your eyes. Bring your attention to your belly, and notice your breathing. If it feels comfortable, breathe through your nose. Breathing through your nostrils for a few breaths naturally slows your pace of breathing, which contributes to slowing your mind. Take as long as you need. When you find you are calm, gently open your eyes, and read the following questions to yourself. Try to answer them as honestly as possible. Be open to new ways of looking at the situation and know that you can revisit it later. This is simply an exploration.

- What dilemma do you currently face in your own life? How might this dilemma be related to your teen and their dilemmas? It might be obscure, but try to find the connection.
- What gifts do you share with your teen? How are you alike?
- Do you communicate subtle expectations of perfection, creating anxiety in you and your teen?
- Are you usually compassionate with your child, but able to suddenly move into "hard-ass" mode and communicate a rigid set of beliefs?
- Are you afraid that when your child no longer needs you, your life may fail to have purpose?
- Are you hyper-focused on an aspect of your teen's life that is a disavowed or unconscious aspect of your own desires?

Now, breathe into your belly to begin to tune into your entire body. Take a moment to imagine yourself being present with your teen. And then in the next moment, imagine your teen walking out the door—saying good-bye. Now imagine a glowing source of light, and allow yourself to experience what it feels like to be connected and aligned with it. Then draw a boundary between yourself and the light. The light is still there, but you are willfully creating distance from it.

Take another breath, and let it out. Imagine your teen speaking disrespectfully to you. What is your reaction? How do you stay connected while also communicating the need for a boundary around your own self?

Some people are more comfortable in living in the paradox; most of us aren't. If you like to journal, take a moment to write about how this exercise went for you. Did anything unexpected come up?

TRANSFORMATION IN PRACTICE: KATE'S STORY

Kate's story is an example of the power of some mighty transformative practices. It is the story of a mother finding profound purpose on a meandering path with much suffering, and ultimately redemption, through and with her teenage son.

Kate told me about her fear and how it had conquered her. Though she was a high-powered lawyer who had pushed through many barriers and conquered significant gender challenges to achieve a high level of professional success, she struggled with matters of the heart. She had also built what I call a "false life" around a set of early childhood wounds. Kate hated her job. Although her life had all the trappings of success, she felt empty. She was significantly depressed, sometimes considered ending her life, and was isolated with few friends and no romantic intimacy. Raising her son largely alone, she had hidden herself away from the world and buried herself in her professional endeavors. Although she had had opportunities to connect to friends and even to lovers, she had taken cover in her work. In the initial session she expressed anger, disgust, and complete intolerance of her eighteen-year-old son, Brian, who had recently failed out of college as a result of substance abuse. "All I can do is cry and feel bitterness about my life," she reported. I told her I was glad she had come in at this crossroads. We had some work to do.

Kate was not unique in experiencing her deepest core wounds activated by her child. Author and psychotherapist John Welwood describes our core wounds as the places of early pain and often trauma.* Kate landed in the chair across from me with a deep sigh of resignation. I knew we were about to unfold a lifetime of pain and challenge over the coming months—packaged in the story of how her son had so profoundly disappointed her. As the tears spilled forth, Kate recounted how Brian had actualized Kate's worst nightmare. Kate spent her life as a single mother focused solely on Brian's education and advancement. Even though she had provided a good life for him, Brian was now addicted to opioids. Kate had a strong intolerance for substance users because of her own family history of substance abuse. As many parents feel at one time or another, Kate had a sinking feeling that all her best efforts at parenting had been a waste of time.

Each session, Kate would say, "I almost didn't come today." As she sat on the couch, choking on her feelings, with streaming tears, her face took on the shape of a disappointed child. "It's just too many feelings. I just can't take it." I told her that unbearable feelings always seem unbearable until we bear them—white knuckling it with a trusted other.

One aspect of moving from a place of imprisonment to a place of liberation is to be brave enough to feel the feelings. This may sound trite or overly simplistic, but it is important to

---

*John Welwood, *Perfect Love, Imperfect Relationships: Healing the Wound of the Heart* (Boston: Shambhala Publications, 2006).

accept the challenge and act on it. The longer the feelings go "unfelt," the more difficult and threatening it is to bring them forward. Kate hadn't truly felt her feelings in many years.

Kate, like many successful patients in my practice, justified a life in which she put her job, money, and status before other more invisible but ultimately more satisfying endeavors like relationships. The authors of *A General Theory of Love* assert that true happiness often comes not from wealth and acquisitions or from the thrill of upward mobility but from the recognition that we depend on each other as humans and that these bonds are ultimately more sustaining than almost anything else. The goal for Kate was to find a life that was sustaining in this way.

Find What's Hidden

Kate's initial set of feelings, expressed as anger over money spent on her son throughout his life, was a metaphor. The surface emotion masked the deep regret she was experiencing. Regret is a strong emotion and is at the root of many of our unresolved feelings about life. Under regret is mourning: the necessary set of feelings one must move through to let go and move on to a new place.

Her son's substance use and the mourning around this event triggered a cascade of grieving experiences, from the loss of Kate's sister as a child to the more remote experience of regret over how she handled her parents' dysfunctional marriage. Session by session I listened as she cried, raged, and shook her fists at the emptiness beside her and inside her. These sessions were interspersed with sessions of great exuberance:

as we freed the negative emotions, the positive could emerge. She wandered and explored: Should she go back to school? Back to work she enjoyed in her twenties working with underprivileged youth? What possibilities might life hold?

Find the Mirror

Additionally, during the next few months, I helped Kate cultivate limit setting as well as compassion for her son. Because she often lapsed into reactive feelings driven by past hurts, this work was difficult. But ultimately, Kate realized that the problems her son experienced coping with emotions—which is why he used substances—were familiar, because Kate also experienced them. Facing her son's maladaptive response helped Kate discover how she had bottled up her own emotions and relied solely on her sharp intellect to boost her successful career.

Slowly she faced the truth about herself: Kate had no friends and was mired in self-loathing. She hadn't engaged in an intimate relationship in years because intimacy requires feeling. Coming to terms with these truths was difficult for her. While her son's severe substance use was an extreme way of medicating pain, Kate was able to see that the fortress she had built around herself was also a dramatic, if more socially acceptable, way to medicate her own pain.

The courage to feel feelings without reaching for something to numb or escape them is an essential practice on the path to healing. Psychology and Buddhism share this belief, as do many other healing and spiritual traditions. The encouragement of the parent, lover, therapist, priest, or shaman can create a holding environment in which it feels safe to feel the feelings. Step by step, we experience each feeling in incremental levels of intensity, until we realize we can survive them. Because of Kate's early wounds, this process was painstaking yet ultimately transformative. Even for a parent who has experienced only minor bumps, the challenges of their teen will rock any vulnerable aspect of them. Because happy and sad emotions are intertwined, the payoff for feeling the dark will be more vibrant and joyful experiences. This allows the parent to fully relish the fun their teen brings to their life together.

We continued to work together to help Kate not react negatively to the horror and what she experienced as the repugnance of her son's use. When we can shift the locus of pain and problems from someone out there—*my teen*—to someone in here—*me*—we can begin to make progress. This meant that Kate had to see that she was beating herself up and had been for many years, and was now doing it in the form of her son.

Find the Self-Love

Some of the most intransigent psychological phenomena are self-hatred and self-criticism. Depression, anxiety, eating disorders, and a host of other issues often result from this pattern. While self-hatred is a complex problem, in good psychotherapy we create awareness of how our self-criticism presents itself so we can begin to dismantle it.

Feelings that cause self-criticism are often unconscious. Once Kate unearthed these feelings and beliefs about herself, her next step was to permit and accept them instead of thinking, "I hate that about myself." I shared an insight from Carl Jung: "What we resist persists." I suggested she reveal and feel. Her world of disavowed feelings and psychic pain slowly shifted to her growing ease in revealing and feeling.

It's important to note that the period of feeling and experiencing a range of emotions was essential to bring Kate to this place of acceptance. We cannot simply overlay an attitude of acceptance onto an emotionally unmetabolized psyche. Many people make this mistake only to revisit the painful feelings again and again.

Once Kate could begin to let the acceptance in, little by little she began to see parallels between the "lies" her son had told her and the "lies" she was tolerating at work. She began to realize that she no longer wished to be part of the hypocrisy in either her personal or her professional life.

Mindfulness Revisited

Especially with teens, it is important to adopt the saying, "Don't believe everything you think." Science is beginning to demonstrate the many benefits of mindfulness, and developing a meditation practice was a key part of Kate's ongoing transformation. I gave her meditations to do twice a day, morning and evening. These sessions allowed her to connect with her Higher Self—that all-knowing, all-loving part of oneself that knows instinctively what is right and how to act.

After many months of meditation and therapy, Kate made the decision to leave her high-powered job to pursue work that was better suited to her skills in a healthy environment that did not repeat her past traumas. Because she had begun to resolve her resentful feelings toward her son and find sources of reward and joy in her own life, her relationship with Brian improved. Her son no longer felt his happiness was the main source of his mother's well-being and felt free to be his imperfect self. As Kate resolved her feelings of self-loathing and instead cultivated self-love, these feelings were naturally extended to Brian.

Not everyone will have the same options Kate did, but we can all make choices about how we choose to react. Once you do the work to see your situation as clearly as possible, you may see options that were previously hidden.

USING SELF-TALK TO DISCOVER SELF

Positive self-talk is a process whereby we identify things that remind us of our worth and boost self-esteem: positive statements like "I know people love me," cards from friends, contacting a loved one, petting a dog, or taking a moment to notice the beauty around you are all examples of this. Once our deep feelings have been acknowledged to some extent, these strategies can allow the positive feelings to grow.

As with the practice of acceptance, I don't suggest that you use these as substitutes for the deeper emotional work you can achieve in therapy. There is a billion-dollar self-help industry that wishes to convince you that if you just tried harder, talked to yourself more, went on another run, or lit another candle, all would be well. While self-help is a step along the way, and many of these techniques can be useful, the application of self-help alone can often lead to more despair. No one is an island. Our deepest troubles are caused by our relationships with those around us; we need to turn to our relationships with trusted humans to heal us.

Used well, positive self-talk can be supportive of deeper work. There are moments for emotional expression and acknowledging the authenticity of our pain—and there are moments when it helps to pivot out of this pain. Positive self-talk exercises are useful as additional tools but should not be seen as the only way to combat self-criticism or any other deeply held emotion.

Talk Back Fears

Kate dreamed of returning to work with women and children. Her life-changing experience doing so years earlier had touched her deeply. Recalling those happy memories penetrated the fortress she had erected to protect her heart. But Kate was fearful and doubtful about the possibilities. "I don't have the money to do that. How would that work logistically?"

When we try to unravel deep patterns and psychic structures, sometimes our fears emerge even more strongly. It's as if those defenses, which developed for a reason, are afraid to leave you undefended. We can see the strength of our emotional traumas in how raw emotions from many years ago can sometimes feel as if they happened yesterday. This was the case for Kate. It was difficult for her to untangle her reality-based fears from her psychic ones.

With practice, she was able to identify which concerns were logistical matters to be overcome and which were actually defensive emotions from her childhood that came back in the form of fear of trying something new. As she began to get better at distinguishing between the two, she got better and better at releasing the fears that stemmed from childhood trauma and not making decisions based on it. We developed ways to "talk back fear." She was able to identify her objections to new opportunities as old, outdated methods of defense. As a result, her life unfolded in ways she never could have imagined.

Though it took the seemingly unbearable pain of her struggle with her son for Kate to dismantle years of crusty emotions and strongly erected defenses, ultimately Kate found her profound purpose.

EXERCISE: FINDING YOUR PURPOSE

- What do you dream of doing? Is there a feeling you are yearning to experience?
- What emotion or experience gets in the way of achieving your goals (e.g., lack of clarity, fear, apathy, guilt about taking time away from your child)?
- How badly do you wish to achieve your goal or find out what you desire?
- If you do have a desire or a purpose that you know but are not pursuing, what are you waiting for?

5

TRANSFORMATIVE STRATEGY #5:
CONTEMPLATE INFINITE POSSIBILITY

T HIS CHAPTER IS ABOUT ENTERTAINING ALL THE OP-
tions that are available to both teens and parents when
they have the peace of mind to explore them. It's about using
our intellect and our spiritual capacities, as well as our emotions, to perceive new opportunities and experiences. So the
daughter perceived as unnecessarily rebellious is instead understood to be the groundbreaking visionary. The son who
has always been disorganized and unfocused is appreciated
for his exquisite compassion and social ease. When you open
yourself to these emotions and experiences, you can appreciate the vastness of your teen's potential, rather than sinking
into habitual patterns of reaction. As you expand your vision
of your teen, new experiences for yourself are also possible.

Charles, father of a precocious fifteen-year-old, struggled to entertain infinite possibility rather than clinging to crisis. In his patterns of control, resisting change, and expecting perfection, neither Charles nor his son had a chance to explore the messy, unpredictable landscapes—both inner and outer—that presented themselves as opportunities for mutual growth. When pushed to explore his own upbringing, Charles entered into a stage of deep grief, as he described his challenging childhood, a time during which his mother made a daily habit of sinking into substance-induced stupor. After exploring these depths, Charles was eventually able to negotiate his son's normal teenage experimentation from a more stable emotional state. Once steady, he was able to realize the vast array of outcomes that could occur beyond his fear-driven scenarios. "Why do I always assume the worst?" Charles would ask, as his son demonstrated time and again that though he was adventurous, he was also trustworthy.

Charles's ability to entertain possibilities for his son's life outside the ones he'd feared helped him to assume the appropriate role of consultant rather than authoritarian. It helped him to listen rather than react.

EMBRACING THE INFINITE: THE ROLE OF ALTERNATIVE HEALING METHODS

I use the term "infinite possibility" as a way of referencing the more subtle aspects of healing that alternative practitioners and Eastern medicine have embraced for millennia with powerful outcomes. While traditional thinkers in the field of psychology, like Jung, wrote extensively about the metaphysical realm (Jung said, "The answer to human life is not to be found within the limits of human life"),[*] Western medicine has been slower to understand and use these practices, even as yoga, meditation, and acupuncture have moved slowly into the mainstream. Thankfully, Western science is catching up to the fact that the mind can and does influence the biomolecular mechanisms involved in body regulation.[†] Some of the exercises I invite patients to practice engage both the physical body and the more "subtle" body: intention, imagination, chakras, and other aspects of the energy body. Thanks to significant research from interdisciplinary fields around the world, the field of alternative medicine is no longer relegated to the "woo-woo" realm. In his famous equation, Einstein predicted the higher dimensional energy field that goes beyond the definition of a human being as a pile of disordered chemicals. This interpretation of $E = mc^2$ embraces what some might call the spiritual dimension of human existence. It says that not only are we physical beings but we are beings of energy, and thus energy can affect us.

EXERCISE: GETTING TO KNOW YOUR CHAKRAS

So let's try an experiment that might push your comfort zone if you're unfamiliar with these alternative methods.

---

[*]C. G. Jung, *Selected Letters of C. G. Jung, 1909–1961* (Princeton, NJ: Princeton University Press, 1984), 25.

[†]For more on this, I recommend Richard Gerber's book *Vibrational Medicine: The #1 Handbook of Subtle-Energy Therapies* (Rochester, VT: Bear & Co., 2001).

All you have to lose is a few minutes of your time, but what you might gain could be valuable in negotiating life with your teen.

The chakras are energetic centers that are thought to be perceptual receptors. You can visualize them as balls of light that are located from the base of your pelvis to the center of your head. Your chakras are where you hold memories and reactions to past experiences. They influence your perception of the present based on which centers you habitually use to assess the world energetically.

The benefits of understanding your chakras can also help you understand the following:[*]

- why you react the way you do.
- where you hold your past.
- why you sometimes feel separate from others.
- that by shifting your perspective, you can experience reality differently.

Like the parts of our physical body, each chakra has a different function. For this exercise, we are going to focus on the first three chakras, because these are the ones that tend to be most triggered when dealing with teens.[†] Our first chakra, at the base of our pelvis, is our creative center (think: sexual creation) and also fear (think: lion hunting you). The second

---

[*]Based on a 2005 lecture from the Foundation for Spiritual Development.

[†]Chris Griscom, *Ecstasy Is a New Frequency: Teachings of the Light Institute* (Santa Fe: Bear & Co., 1987).

chakra is in the lower abdomen, and it's about what people think of us and informs our sense of our identity. Our third chakra sits within the solar plexus, and is where we hold judgment and clear discrimination.

Chakras are like the lens of a camera; they open and close in relation to the energy that is in them and radiating from them. With awareness, we can bring attention to these energy centers and emphasize or palpate from them. For example, to become more grounded and in touch with our creativity and sexual center, we can bring awareness and energy to the first chakra in the area of the base of the spine and genitals. If we wish to communicate with more spiritual, less physical aspects of ourselves and life, the third eye (located on the forehead between the eyebrows) and the chakra just above the head may be channels to these types of experiences. Meditation is often a good means to becoming more familiar with these channels.

Let's experiment with another strategy for letting go— one from the "alternative" world. If it doesn't work for you, that's fine. At least you tried. Close your eyes, and take a deep breath. Let it out slowly. Now imagine that you are sitting inside a golden, glowing ball. Once you're inside this place, I want you to think about a conflict you're having with your teen.

Scan your body. Where is the conflict living? What part of your body feels alive, afraid, activated, stuck, heavy, or otherwise? Are you aware of feeling judged as a parent? Judgmental of your teen? That would be your third chakra, right in your sternum. Are you obsessed with how obsessed your daughter is with her appearance? Second chakra—just around your belly button. Utter fear of some terrible accident, your teen's fate? An impending catastrophe? That's the first chakra, right at your seat.

Noticing where in your body you register reactions and feelings about your teen allows you to go to this place—your stomach, your throat, your head—to release the feelings and energy stored there. As Peter Levine, an expert in healing trauma through what he calls "Somatic Experiencing," writes in his seminal work *Waking the Tiger*, "Body and mind, primitive instincts, emotions, intellect and spirituality all need to be considered together in studying the organism." In other words, "it's all energy."[*]

This exercise addresses the physiological aspects of holding onto emotion. It brings the mind to the body to clear the energy stored there. Let's say you've identified a place in your body where an emotion, perhaps anger, is living. Maybe you feel it in your throat. Allow yourself to visualize this anger vividly. And then, to bring the power of the mind to heal this place, imagine bringing in liquid light, or a color, or just breathing into your throat to touch that felt experience of anger. Whether it be a color, a light, a breath, or an image, allow this other energy to superimpose itself on this place of pain. By doing so, you are allowing your Higher Self to support you with healing painful emotions.

---

[*]Peter Levine, *Waking the Tiger: Healing Trauma* (Berkeley: North Atlantic Books, 1997), 8, 109.

CULTIVATE SELF-LOVE AND COMPASSION

Possibilities always start from within. When we know our issues and triggers, we can truly begin to cultivate self-love and compassion that then translate to our teen. Teens are in search of authenticity—not just in themselves but in us. Any trace of self-hatred will end up being projected onto them as self-criticism. Because teens' identities are wobbly, self-criticism doesn't feed the bonds of love and trust. It erodes those bonds that are so necessary for cultivating a good relationship. Many parents I work with wish that I could help their teens manage their emotions when the parents themselves are using substances, a too-busy life, or other distractions to numb their own emotional capacity and general functioning. Other parents simply need an expanded understanding of their own character and their teen's to solve the struggles they encounter.

One mother came to me because she was having trouble navigating her thirteen-year-old daughter's severe mood swings. "She used to be the perfect child. I can't handle this!" She couldn't see any possibility other than a complete downward spiral into total failure for her daughter. But her daughter's volatility was fueled, in part, by her mother's inability to imagine any other outcome. The mother's own self-described "even-keeled" personality did not contain the possibility of strong anger, sadness, or tantrums like the ones her daughter was now presenting. In sessions with the mother, I invited her to consider her daughter's very different character and the possibility that she would be alright despite the current state of crisis.

Self-love, as it relates to our teens, requires self-examination and self-expansion. Without our own growth in these areas, we risk becoming locked into our own limited judgments—and locking our teens into them as well. Arguments and power struggles are often signals that we as parents could benefit from an elaborated view of what we hold to be reality.

EXERCISE: QUESTIONS TO CLEAR SPACE AND CREATE NEW OPPORTUNITIES

So let's engage in extraordinary thinking and push our imagination to create infinite possibility! Take a moment to get comfortable and take a few breaths. Then invite *all* aspects of your being, the physical, emotional, and spiritual aspects, to show up. If the term "spiritual" puts you off, try "energetic." This is an experiment. If it doesn't work, then stay with the physical aspects by being mindful of your emotions and your thoughts.

Consider the following questions:

- **What buttons is my teen pressing in me today?** Is there an inner child, a young set of emotions, moving inside to speak to me about these buttons? Is there a neglected eight-year-old? A teen whose dad didn't acknowledge her? A young adult who was afraid to launch a life so instead had an eating disorder or an addiction? A young man who had to stuff his emotions to "grow up" and take on responsibility? A child who was neglected or traumatized?

- **Is there one set of buttons that may become a tunnel to the treasure?** Is there a place of fear that can be transformed to sustain the bond between me and my teen? For example, is my daughter talking so much and playing the role of the drama queen so that I can be given the opportunity to take a break from my type A life and slow down long enough to listen? Or is my son pushing far outside the box, engaging in dangerous behaviors, so that I might have the chance to look at some of my rigidly "in the box" approaches to life and grow a bit? Is my teenage daughter mired in emotional intensity because I have lived a life of skimming over, minimizing, or ignoring the deep wells of my own emotional being? Is my son chaotic so I can face my own fears about chaos?
- **How can I expand?** What possibilities can I entertain about myself and about my teen?

TRANSFORMATION IN PRACTICE: LILY AND SIENNA

Lily, a mother who had struggled with very limiting beliefs about her own life and thus about the life of her daughter, Sienna, arrived at one of our sessions uncharacteristically cheerful and at ease. We were about halfway through the full treatment cycle, and she said that our work together to reframe her life was finally making sense. She had played the role of caretaker to her mother while growing up, and I had suggested that even though in the past she had taken care of others and still felt obligated to do so, she didn't need to continue to live that way. She was understanding and accepting of my strong urging to live her own life.

Of course, these realizations came through a long iterative process involving some of the earlier principles described in this book. But eventually, Lily put space between her old life and the present day so she could create a new, vital life that reflected her current state of mind. While still working in her sales job for income, she went back to school at night to study biology, her original passion. She planned a trip to South America with the intention of assisting in an ongoing botany project there.

As Lily's possibilities broadened, her eighteen-year-old daughter, Sienna, who had been using marijuana and had self-described her life as "stalled," began attending regular Narcotics Anonymous meetings for her substance problem and attending her own therapy. In our meetings, Sienna spoke about how witnessing her mother's "revival" had motivated her to infuse her own life with new meaning.

It makes sense that teenagers will be inspired by revolution, because it is the central activity of the teenage brain to contemplate infinite possibility. As psychiatrist Daniel Siegel found:

> The key to creative solution was honoring the natural adolescent drive for innovation and the creation of new ways of doing things. Honoring does not mean setting no

limits. It means acknowledging the intention behind the action. Adolescence is all about experimentation. If adults shut that down, the passion for novelty will be thwarted, the teens will become disillusioned and disconnected, and no one will benefit.[*]

Parents need only allow this capacity to unfold. Where I see parents getting in the way is when their teen's creative solutions do not align with the parents' ideas about creativity or solutions. Honoring the essence of your teen's expansion no matter how it looks, within limits but with as much possible flexibility on your part, will generate the most possibilities for relationship and reward for both of you.

WITHDRAWING PROJECTIONS

Projections are feelings we have about ourselves that we unconsciously ascribe to others. Easy to spot in others but difficult to see in ourselves, our children are the perfect vessel for our projections. Does our son seem lazy because we aren't as successful as we think we should be? Does our concern about our own social standing make our daughter's desire to retreat to her room for more alone time seem unbearable? Because we are usually unaware of our projections, they are difficult to manage. If we are irritable, unhappy, or otherwise unfulfilled, how easy is it for us to see our teen's slouching at the table, isolation, lack of physical prowess, low grades,

---

[*]Daniel J. Siegel, *Brainstorm: The Power and Purpose of the Teenage Brain* (New York: Tarcher/Penguin, 2013), 270.

or any number of behaviors or situations as cause for stress and recrimination?

The truth is that the outside world will always cause us pain if we allow it. Of course, there are objective challenges in life—more for some than for others. But it's how we interpret and react to life's pain that determines our quality of experience and how intensely we experience objectively painful situations. As parents begin to withdraw their projections and look inward rather than solely at their teen for the solution, their lives begin to change.

EXERCISE: UNMASKING HIDDEN PROJECTIONS

Brainstorm a list of possible projections you might be putting on your teen. These may include fears you have about them (which are reflections of fears you have about yourself) or ideas about who you wish they would become or who you think they *should* become. Projections may take the form of a relative or someone you dislike ("You are exactly like your father!"). In relationships full of conflict, or with divorce, it is common for a parent to project the disliked "other" parent onto their child without even realizing it. This projection can be particularly painful for a teenager who feels that if he shows the part of himself that is like, for example, his father, he will lose his mother's love.

Think about it. Once you notice these projections, I invite you to become conscious of them so that you needn't burden your teen with them.

TRANSFORMATION IN PRACTICE: COLIN'S STORY

Colin was a thirteen-year-old boy with depression and attention deficit disorder. Both parents came to me exasperated, especially his mom, Rebecca, who said, "He is so attention-seeking and manipulative, I can't take it anymore." Her candor was necessary; it's important that we be honest about how our children affect us, the good and the bad. It can be difficult to acknowledge how stressful it is to be a parent, or how annoying or sometimes even threatening our children can be. But if we cannot be honest, we cannot truly see the openings for new behavior.

As I worked with Rebecca, what emerged was her abusive father's chronic criticism of her for the same problems. As a teen, she was the class clown, a clever creative girl who wanted to make people laugh. Her parents were critical of her behavior and quashed any hopes of this aspect of her growing and thriving. Through many sessions we moved through the emotions, like shame, sadness, and anger, that were contained in her strong condemnations of her own son. At times it felt as if her beliefs were so solid that they would never change. But as she felt the feelings, Rebecca was able to see more clearly that her judgments about Colin were a result of her own deep wounds.

Once aware, she began to shift her attitude toward her son. As she became aware of how and why her son triggered her, she began to allow room for the silly side of his personality to take form, and concurrently, Colin's depression improved.

The beauty of possibility: with her own shame cleared, she could appreciate the aspects of Colin that she could never appreciate in herself.

As Rinpoche, citing Shantideva, an eighth-century Buddhist monk, wrote, "If the land were full of sharp stones and thorns, you might try to protect your feet by covering over the whole countryside with tough leather. But that would be a difficult task. It is much easier to put the leather just on the soles of your feet."

Practice Acceptance

The moment you accept a situation, you begin to change your feelings as well as your thoughts. Your ability to respond rather than react increases. This is a yogic as well as psychological principle and could be considered central to many healing traditions. It's important to note that this can only happen after working through difficult emotions. The period of experiencing a range of emotions is essential to bringing yourself to this place of acceptance. The valuable practices of gratitude and acceptance are less effective when we're in significant emotional pain, conflict, or turmoil. Emotions can change incrementally, and the process of change is iterative, meaning that it usually requires you to revisit your wounds again and again and to make multiple discoveries before the insight stays with you. Even as you step forward, you are always looping back, so don't be discouraged if you find yourself thinking, "This again! I thought I was done grieving (or being angry or feeling intensely) over this!" Many people make the mistake of forcing acceptance only to revisit painful feelings again and again. As a parent you must spend time with your anger, your dark side, the earlier parts of your upbringing, in order to begin the process of accepting yourself and your teen.

Practice Gratitude

Cultivating the infinite possibilities in both ourselves and our teens requires space in our minds and in our emotional being. We all know that when we are distracted, too busy, stressed, or holding heavy emotions, our field of options becomes narrow. Practicing gratitude is another activity that opens the doors of possibility because it gives us the immediate experience of ease: "I am enough; my teen is enough."

Science is now demonstrating what spiritual teachers have known for millennia: an ongoing, sustained practice of gratitude is central to positive mental health. Keeping a gratitude journal, saying thanks a few times a day, or just turning our minds toward what we have rather than thinking about what we lack is a simple action that can reap great rewards.

Ask yourself at least once a day, "As a parent, what am I thankful for?" It's so easy to feel that we or our children are somehow not living up to some preconceived ideal, and our teens pick up on this. Many of the adolescents in my practice report that they can just "sense" their parents' disappointment. "They say they only care if I do my best, and then they ask me why I got a B. That confuses me and makes me feel like I can never live up to their expectations." There is nothing worse than a teen who feels he cannot satisfy us. Our children pick up on the tiniest signs of our disappointment; they are biologically wired to be exquisitely tuned into us.

Because we have known our children all their lives, it can be difficult to see the many possibilities for more positive interaction and growth that can emerge if we change the habits of our mind.

OUR TEEN: EMBODYING THE INFINITE AND THE FINITE

Jung wrote eloquently about the truth and power of paradox.[*] In order to move from crisis to infinite possibility, we must learn how to contain opposites. We must sharpen our inner vision in order to see the developmental paradox before us: our teenager vacillating from child to adult from one moment to the next, back and forth. And we must continue the process of looking within, even in the face of discomfort and fear, for how else are we to grow? The more we embrace infinite possibility, the more we know that we will blossom, not despite the challenges our teens present but because of them.

---

[*]Jung, *Selected Letters*, 121.

6

TRANSFORMATIVE STRATEGY #6:
HEAL THYSELF

*When the senses are stilled, when the mind is at rest, when the
intellect wavers not—then, say the wise, is reached the highest stage.
This steady control of the sense and mind has been defined as Yoga.*

—B. K. S. Iyengar

B. K. S. IYENGAR HAS BEEN DESCRIBED BY MANY AS THE
father of yoga. His definition of yoga had little to do
with the crowded studios and luxury "lifestyle" products of
today; instead it emphasized the yoking of mind and body.
When you penetrate to the truth within yourself to interact with your teen, you are also doing the work of yoga—of
connecting. You cannot possibly expect to have an authentic
relationship with your teen if you do not have an authentic
relationship with yourself. And your emotions are the signals,

the maps to that place of truth within you. In this chapter you will go even deeper into the emotions that shape your reactions, so that you can emerge with healing for yourself and effective strategies for your teen.

When you become a parent, you develop a new aspect of your intelligence that involves your ability to adapt to change and to develop inner resources to ensure the survival and health of your children. And while our culture is preoccupied with happiness, focusing on the positive and denying all that is not bright and shiny, more mature cultures acknowledge both the yin and the yang, seeing the darkness to experience the light. This is the nature of true health and contentment. Our planet and the ecosystems around us rely on cycles of decay and renewal, and so do we. As we continue to learn about the importance of biodiversity, one of the world's leading biologists and experts in ecological science reminds us, "We need to reframe the concept of decomposition into regeneration."* What does rotting have to do with parenting? I highlight this biological parallel because I think it's easier for people to grasp the importance of decomposition and regeneration in relation to the Earth than it is for them to see their own dark sides. And yet what they would rather not see may actually be the most valuable asset to their growth as humans and to their success as parents.

Not long ago I worked with a client whose relationship with his teenage son was threatened by the recent US presidential election. Rob was unable to hear anything his more

---

*From an interview with Paul Stamets in *Common Ground* magazine, March 2007.

liberal sixteen-year-old son, Darren, had to say about his beliefs. The son insisted that his father's support of Trump was a deal breaker; he refused to talk to him. What was once a close and nourishing bond was fraying. Father and son came to me in crisis: their relationship was on the line.

The aim of my work as a psychotherapist is to repair my clients' ability to love in the face of what seem like impossible challenges. This healing takes us deep into ourselves by way of the limbic system. Can our identification with political beliefs topple the most essential human bonds, even one as primal as father and son? How do we repair the lost love between a parent and a child? When we hit core places like identity—which politics and religion often touch—we need to go deeper than usual in order to open space. We may not want to, but we need to do this work because as mammals, relationships matter. I believe that healing the bond between an alienated teen and his parent is the first step to healing the collective wounds of the world. It is slow-going and sometimes meandering work, but any repair to this primal bond is worth the effort.

When I am working with any dyad—be it parent/child, husband/wife, or otherwise—I ask both members to take a moment to go within and see where they are being touched emotionally. Where is the rigidity or pain coming from? Then I invite the person who identifies as being the least "wounded," or who has the least complex set of painful issues *in that moment*, to start to create space and flexibility. Ideally both will bend and flex a bit, but this can be difficult, if not impossible, at times.

This father/son pair did not want their relationship to perish over Trump. So at least we had that common ground to start from. What Rob needed to bring forth was his fear of being vulnerable. As he sat and raged over his son criticizing him, he stomped his foot a few times as an exclamation point. I saw this physical symptom as a somatic window to his emotions.

"What are you feeling when you stomp your foot?" I asked. Rob looked surprised and then solemn. He took a moment before revealing to me the deep vow he had made as a child when he was bullied by his cruel stepfather: never back down. "You have to defend yourself in life," he explained. "I stand behind my beliefs. No one walks on me." His inner child had spoken.

YOUR INNER CHILD HAS SOMETHING TO SAY

Though the term "inner child" has become part of the mainstream, some people may balk at it. I have found it to be a powerful metaphor that has helped create significant transformation for many of my clients—so powerful that it is worth revisiting from different angles throughout this book. So even if it feels unfamiliar to you, I invite you to go out on a limb and explore how it might illuminate an aspect of your psyche that has heretofore been in the dark.

Emotions can be arrested in their development by trauma, neglect, or a combination of both, thereby preventing us from growing and adapting to the world around us. Different developmental stages correlate with different styles of defense, pain, and constellations of symptoms. For example, a child who has trauma or neglect around age two, the age of differentiation and separation, may experience some version of separation anxiety as an adult. So we can use the term "inner child" as shorthand for a stage where a person may have become stuck in their emotional growth. Inviting the inner child to take form and speak is a handy tool to go back in time and talk about this place that often doesn't get articulated but rather is repressed, denied, or acted out—often with your teen.

As Rob stomped his foot for the third time I asked him to pause and feel the fighter. "I don't want to fight with my son," he said, choking back tears. A few escaped down his flushed cheek.

"I know you don't," I said.

For Rob to accept his son's criticism of him, a key aspect of parenting, he had to face deep feelings that had never been revealed—shame, guilt, lack of self-love, to name a few. For him to heal he needed to go to these earlier wounds.

My listening to Rob describe his old wounds helped him to make space for his son's beliefs without feeling threatened. When I looked over at Darren, he seemed to be engaged with his father for the first time in a long while. He even reached over to touch his father's knee.

"Do you have to keep fighting?" I asked.

Rob nodded, tears still flowing: the tears of his inner child knowing that he didn't have to fight anymore. They were tears of relief, of empathy for his own pain. A softness emerged as his eyes and body settled, and that softness extended into empathy for his son.

"I love my son," he said. "That's the bottom line. Who cares if he criticizes me? He's a teenager. He needs to have his opinions heard, too. I'm his dad. I can just listen."

"Yes, you can," I said with a renewed sense of confidence that father and son had reentered each other's hearts, where they belonged.

EXERCISE: HEALING YOUR INNER CHILD

This is an exercise to identify and begin to heal your inner child so it doesn't have to interfere with your relationship with your teen. Sit back. Take a deep breath, and let it out slowly. Begin to feel your way into a conflict you are currently having with your adolescent. Maybe it's about her attitude. Perhaps he is not respecting his curfew. Or maybe your daughter is choosing to spend time with the boyfriend you can't stand rather than joining in family activities.

Whatever behavior is triggering you at this time, notice the feeling state it stirs in you. A "feeling state" is a combination of feelings or a fluid, shifting set of related feelings. So you could be feeling sad, lonely, abandoned. Or angry and hopeless. Whatever it is, I want you to now use your emotion stethoscope, which, like a stethoscope used by a doctor, discerns the internal signals of the body. Rather than probing the state of the heart and lungs, this stethoscope, the data from which are equally important for your emotional survival, discerns the physical features of feeling states in your body—tight, soft, fluttery, tar-like, painful-like-knives-cutting—so you can feel them with more intensity and experience all their nuances. You can only make conscious what you know in great detail. Your imaginary stethoscope invites you to gather data about the somatic aspects of your emotional life.

Once you've identified these feelings in exquisite detail, see if you can travel back to find your first experience with this particular set of feelings. Again, this isn't easy work. But if you spend a few minutes and answer the questions below, you will be closer to having an authentic relationship with your teen than you were before this exercise.

- How old are you?
- What are you wearing?
- Where are you? (A room in your house? At school? In a field?)
- What is going on in your life with other family members, particularly your mother and father?
- What's your narrative about life at this time? (e.g., "No one is ever there for me" or "Don't feel these feelings; just shut them out and move on.")
- Once you have identified your earlier experiences with these feelings, inquire into your specific bodily sensations. For example, where in your body are you feeling empty and sad? Can you sense more subtle aspects of this experience? Is the feeling still or moving? Hot?

Thick? What does that feeling actually look like as you feel it? What images emerge from the feeling? Buzzing bees? An empty box? A cold landscape? Are the feelings intense or subtle?

Now come back to the current time, and ask yourself as the adult to nurture and comfort your inner child. Imagine you are talking to a child, a friend, or anyone to whom you have the experience of expressing tenderness and compassion. Is there a way you can reframe the situation or a concept that counters the inner child's firm belief in her feeling state? This may be difficult; don't be discouraged. If you can't figure out how to comfort your inner child, simply imagine what that child needs at this moment from a trusted other. You may not be able to give it to her right now. But at least she can express herself, and you as the adult can listen. Don't hurry her along. Take your time.

And then when you are ready, open your eyes, and come back to the present.

TRANSFORMATION IN PRACTICE: JOHN'S INNER AND OUTER CHILD

John, a well-meaning dad of an older teen, was ready to get in contact with his inner child in order to improve his relationship with his son. But as he started to summon this younger part of himself, he found his first reactions were ones of revulsion, anger, and shame. Like many of my patients, he didn't want to connect with this part of himself. The work was slow.

First I had him imagine tolerating this child as you would a feral cat: you give it some milk (some love), and you wait. The inner child begins to take shape.

At last he was ready to introduce this child to me. He described this younger part of himself as a little boy with glasses, short brown hair, and a quiet fearful demeanor. He lived in a small room with a collection of matchbox cars. While young John admitted that life in this small room was limited, he preferred it to the outside world because it was predictable and under his complete control. John was able to develop a dialogue with this little boy, and eventually his inner child felt safe enough to leave the small room with adult John beside him as his trusted guide.

This is slow, painstaking, yet ultimately deeply rewarding work because it puts us squarely in relationship to the deepest seeds of our emotional illusions. That's where the action is. This courageous journeying mirrored John's growing flexibility with his son, Sam.

Before his inner child work, John was unable to tolerate any pain his son experienced. John would obsessively read text messages on Sam's phone in order to make sure he wasn't hanging out with the "bad crowd." His desire to protect Sam was disallowing his son the growth exploration that is necessary to being a teenager.

John is not alone in confusing his inner child with his real child. Most parents live their lives in this unexamined way. Children arrive and fill unmet needs, receive projections, and suffer the confusion of this mix-up with varying degrees of success. We are more likely to suffer sleepless nights, panic, and confusion when our inner child remains a mystery. I invite my parent clients to take this deep journey inward because when they get to the heart of the matter of their inner child, they are more likely to penetrate to the heart of the matter of their outer—their real—child. And consequently they are better able to be present and empathize with their teen.

As John healed his own inner child and then his inner teen, he no longer had to project his issues onto Sam. The more he was able to trust Sam, the more steps Sam made toward becoming trustworthy, and the more Sam was able to make empowered decisions about his own social interactions. With a newly enlarged capacity to tolerate both his own pain and his son's, John's autocratic behavior yielded to calm conversations during which he could invite his Higher Self to discuss with his son how Sam could take care of himself in situations in which others might present him with risks that weren't in his best interest. John's conversations with Sam about alcohol shifted from angry, authoritative demands of sobriety to dialogues during which he would invite Sam to author his own relationship to substances. He asked good questions, gave Sam his family history, and, rather than lecturing, invited Sam's own developing reason and maturity to make decisions.

The idea of trust can be foreign when it isn't felt and experienced day to day in your family of origin. Often it is not until you move into the dark regions of pain and fear and then reemerge as the adult self that you can truly guide your teen. Giving your kids the tools to make their own best decisions isn't as easy as telling them what to do, but ultimately it is more effective.

HOW TO GO INWARD IN AN OUTWARD-FACING CULTURE

We live in a culture of action over reflection. There are many fruits of action, but if we don't balance action with the slower yet powerful processes of introspection, meditation, and understanding the ways of our own psyches, we can end up, as one patient put it, "feeling like I'm running alongside of my life, rather than living it."

In his book *Thank You for Being Late*, Thomas Friedman echoes these concerns about the dizzying speed of technology. He chronicles our culture's recent acceleration and concludes that a particular type of slowness—one that requires us to ignore the noise to access our deepest values—is the tonic. He concludes that creating connection and community and slowing down are some of the remedies for this new generation. I agree. The exercises and ideas I provide are based on a certain kind of empathic tuning in. This tuning in is focused and particular; it takes you deeply inside yourself so that you can bring out what is truly valuable to the world around you. The world needs this part of all of us.

From what I have witnessed about healing in my practice, we need to grow internally, emotionally, and in our consciousness as swiftly as we are living externally. Our current engagement with the world (through the internet, globalization, and fast everything) can be described as horizontal growth; now we need to go vertical—deep inside ourselves. In an interview

Steve Huffman, the thirty-four-year-old founder and CEO of Reddit, described how "technology alters our relations to one another, for better and for worse." He has witnessed how social media can magnify public fears. "It's easier for people to panic when they're together. . . . Our technologies have made us more alert to risk, but have also made us more panicky; they facilitate the tribal temptation to cocoon, to seclude ourselves from opponents and to fortify ourselves against our fears instead of attacking the sources of them."[*]

Fear is the biological wiring that makes you as a parent care more than anything else about what is happening moment to moment with your child. Coupled with your own emotional struggles that may be unresolved, this adaptive emotion can be a place of constriction, reaction, and tension that limits your decision making and narrows the field of options you have to use to manage the complex dilemmas your teen presents to you. How do you manage the deep fear that strikes in your bones during these, and less extreme, events throughout your child's life? Sometimes the fear comes in the form of catastrophic scenarios that keep you up at night. Fear lurks and pounces unless you have an orientation to your own psyche, an understanding of your triggers and strategies to soothe the body and mind. The only emotion that rivals the joy you feel as a parent is deep concern. The necessary emotions that drive adolescents' growth is desire for freedom, to discover their identity. Teens are nearly fearless! It's the oxygen they need to live during

---

[*]Evan Osnos, "Doomsday Prep for the Super-Rich," *New Yorker*, January 30, 2017.

this period of tremendous growth and exploration. Your trust in your teen's ability to be an adult is their currency. As one teen put it, "When they don't believe me, or trust me, I completely shut them out." Imagine what it's like when someone doesn't understand your most essential and precious mission. How do you react?

FINDING YOUR "TYPE"

Self-knowledge plays an important role in healing ourselves and healing our teens.

While each parent is an individual comprised of their own set of strengths and vulnerabilities, I have found that if you can identify some general clusters of behaviors, you can begin to access your strengths. Read about the six parent types below, and see if any feel familiar to you. Perhaps one type doesn't exactly describe your style; you may be an amalgamation of several. But in reviewing these types, you may find a familiar quality that will spark a recognition and subsequently a more thorough knowledge of yourself. These characterizations aren't meant to limit you but to raise awareness so that you can grow beyond them and "heal thyself."

THE MICROMANAGER: "Text me when you get to Johnny's." Sound familiar? While overseeing your teen's life and making sure they are safe is important, it's most effective in moderation. A question to ask yourself if you think you might be a Micromanager is: What is my relationship, in general, to control? Does spontaneity fill me with delight or dread? Does the unknown about anything spike anxiety that sometimes is hard to handle? If you answered yes to these questions, actively choosing to engage in situations that are not under your control and characterized by the unknown may begin to heal this aspect of your emotional self.

THE WARRIOR: Do you feel hurt when your teen pushes you away? Do you take everything personally? Do you start arguments about behaviors that are developmentally appropriate for teens—like being a bit fresh, living in their bedroom, or telling white lies? Anger is a cover for hurt. So the more aggressive you find yourself in response to any aspect of your teen's life, the more it would benefit you to examine the vulnerabilities that you may be ignoring. The Warrior is the parent who, to their credit, overrides their emotions much of the time and carries on. They get a lot done. These are strengths—in moderation. If you find yourself picking up the sword for battle in response to minor provocations from your teen, it may be time to cultivate a relationship with your softer side. Know that the capacity to conquer does not feed the capacity for compassion. Rent some movies that make you cry, take long walks in nature, or spend time with friends with whom you can let your guard down. Get out of your head and into your heart.

THE WORRIER: Is the sky falling perpetually for you? Do you feel worried about every aspect of your teen's life? Do you catastrophize aspects of your teen's life that may involve some risk but that are basically safe? Most parents worry; this is normal. I am referring here to chronic overreaction to a teen's normal everyday activities that should only elicit normal anxiety: driving, refusing to let us know where they are for a period of time, experimentation with substances, and so forth. Worriers need discipline to curb the creation of catastrophic scenarios. Meditation is an essential tool. Exercise for anxiety is a basic self-care activity. Understanding and working through the early roots of your anxiety with a therapist helps. An active spiritual life is also beneficial, whether it's a formal religious activity or gathering with a group of parents to sing or dance. Doing so can connect you to the larger mysteries, thus allowing the Worrier to put her concerns about her teen in proper proportion.

THE PROJECTER: "You remind me of . . ." Does your teen remind you of your ex-husband, whom you despise? Or do their behaviors trigger memories of someone else in your past whom you fear they will grow into? Do you project your general fears about life onto your teen? Or do you project some of the good parts of yourself onto your child? "She will be a basketball star"; "he is so clever at math, just like me." Again, there is nothing wrong with supporting your child in developing characteristics or pursuing activities that you favor and that are similar to your own traits or activities you enjoy. It's when it is a complete mismatch to your teen's natural personality that problems arise. This type of projecting is a defense that usually comes from fear. Like most defenses, it is often unconscious, which is why it is difficult to notice and change. If you are a parent who naturally thinks you are usually (always?) right and your teen is always wrong, you may use projection as your defense of choice. And it's easy to do! Because teens are experimenting, they often *are* wrong and stumble into gigantic messes. Putting our thoughts, fears, and imaginings on our teen is a surefire way to alienate them. The Projecting Parent benefits from turning the focus away from his teen and toward himself. Ask yourself: What am I not feeling? Who am I afraid to be? What am I resisting?

THE PERFECTIONIST: Is nothing ever enough? Do you find that you are disappointed in many aspects of your teen's behaviors? Disappointed parents can come from many places emotionally. Perhaps your teen is very different from you—you were the good girl, and she's the rebel—and you just can't get your head around it. Maybe you are naturally a "glass half empty" person whose teen is now shining the light on this part of your personality and inviting you to see the good in life and in your child. Being disappointed with your teen, even if you don't say so, will only serve to alienate them from you because, even when they don't show it, they usually still care about your approval.

THE DREAMER: Do you have unconscious expectations that are impossible to be met by your teen (or anyone)? Is there a sense that your teen should fulfill dreams and goals that you never fulfilled yourself? That you wish you had? Holding aspirations for your child is one of the joys of parenting—until it becomes excessive or exaggerated. Because your teen is a mirror of yourself, you find that you have these ideas of grandeur in the other areas of your life as well. Your boss just isn't appreciative enough; your job doesn't completely maximize your talents or pay you enough; your teen is missing a sense of something, but you're not sure what. Look within yourself, and find the core of that incessant push to exceed expectations. Maybe you are enough. And maybe your teen is too.

All six of these types have at their root the desire for their child to be safe, happy, and successful. Even the desire that your child surpasses you in some way is a natural parental instinct. But when these goals are unrealistic for your teen's capacities, or come from an unfulfilled part of you that seeks expression through your teen's life instead of your own, they aren't entirely healthy. A good question to ask yourself if you find yourself needing your child to play a certain role: Is this for them, or is this for you?

CULTURAL HEALING: ADJUSTING YOUR EXPECTATIONS OF YOUR TEEN

Riku was a thirteen-year-old Japanese American boy who was brought into my office by his parents because he no longer enjoyed spending time with them and was pushing back on schoolwork and other responsibilities. His mother explained in our first session, "We used to enjoy so many things together. Now he listens to loud, aggressive music in his room." Born and raised in Japan and now living in the

United States, both parents expressed to me their fear that their boy would adopt what they considered the depraved and overly individualistic aspects of American culture. They had not expressed this to Riku directly. Instead, they had tried to woo him back into activities with them that would reinforce his Japanese roots and discourage his independence.

It is not my role to interfere with cultural values that parents wish to transmit to their children. What I do is illuminate the most effective ways that parents can stay connected to their teen, which allows them to continue their relationship in the most satisfying manner. Riku's parents were not unlike other parents of young teens in that they needed some education about the difference between nine-year-olds and thirteen-year-olds. But these parents had the added layer of fear about their son abandoning their cultural values and being drawn into what they deemed to be a less healthy set of cultural norms. This unconscious conflict needed to be unearthed and managed, or Riku would be destined to overly embrace American culture to "win" this unconscious power struggle.

Once his parents understood the normal separation behaviors of young teens and were invited to have a dialogue with Riku about their values—that included space for Riku to express his own conflicts about having two different cultural influences—all were able to find equilibrium. In our last session, his mother reported that Riku invited her into his room at night and asked her to listen to the music he was now interested in. And while she often had to bite her tongue, she instinctively knew that by being with Riku through his experimentation, she had a greater chance of supporting him to find the healthy aspects of both cultures than if she tried to enforce rules about how he should engage.

This exchange is yet another example of the importance of finding the unspoken and the unconscious, so that your teen does not have to express it. Through these challenges with Riku, his parents were able to heal their own fears about integrating into a different culture. Their shift in attitude illuminated the satisfaction of staying in a relationship with their son rather than choosing to alienate him.

COMMUNICATION IS NOT JUST WHAT WE SAY

Human beings only communicate about 10 percent verbally. This means that most of the cues we pick up from each other are transmitted and received nonverbally. What does this mean for you and your teen?

Parents will often say, "I never told my child about my past." Or, "I never told them that my dreams included X." Or even, "I've never told him how disappointed I have been in him." But because they are so exquisitely attached to and dependent on us, our children don't need us to consciously, explicitly let them know who we are. They read it in every glance, every word, every feeling, and that builds a pattern over the years. It's amazing to me how many teens I work with replicating patterns that their parents lived, whether it's problems related to food, drug use, sexual promiscuity, or the opposite, such as becoming a high achiever, a wonderful dancer, or a caring nurse. There is nothing wrong with this imitation by our children; it is altogether natural. I point it out because many parents think that it is only what they say explicitly, and demonstrate consciously, that their children follow. This couldn't be less true. If you care about what your teen is taking in from you, it is beneficial to know both what you show consciously and what you reveal unconsciously.

When we do the deeper work, we unwind these invisible threads that communicate things without us knowing. These unconscious messages aren't always bad. But being conscious about what we are communicating usually yields better results all around.

CONFLICT: ANOTHER WAY TO CONNECT

Warm relationships should always be a goal, as they sustain us and tend to be our biggest sources of important memories. But sometimes, in the absence of these types of relationships, there are other ways parents and teens attempt to connect.

We know that negative attention can seem better than no attention. I work with many families who are experiencing a high level of conflict, which, of course, is ultimately divisive. But in some cases, when parents have had either traumatic or negligent early lives, their teens create conflict as one way of generating connection. In these cases, therapy is important for the parents. But even for parents who have had more "normal" upbringings, time to connect can be challenging and compromised. In this age of dual-income families, along with the ability to work or be on a device at all times, how do parents connect to themselves and to their teens? What is the quality of that connection? How difficult is it to put aside the phone or computer?

Often our children are angry or demanding because it is the only way to force us to disengage from the distraction and engage with *them*. Finding focused, undistracted time is not easy, but it's necessary if we wish to nourish important bonds. As we come to the end of this chapter, I urge you to ask yourself these questions:

- Are my teen and I unconsciously connecting through conflict?
- Do we have healthy ways of connecting, or are we too busy or preoccupied to truly connect?
- How do I emotionally connect to myself? To my teen?
- What is my inner child's narrative? And what does that child need in order to feel heard and healed?

Having relationships requires the highest level of healing thyself, because if you are unhappy and do not love yourself, how can you expect to find happiness and love in relationship? Harvard's famous seventy-five-year longitudinal study demonstrated what therapists and your grandma have always known: have good, warm relationships, and you will be successful. Not only that, you will live longer. At the end of the day, and at the end of your life, relationships are what really matter. Connecting with your teen and modeling a life of healthy connection are two of the very best things you can do as a parent.

ATTACHMENT QUOTIENT (AQ)

I have come up with the term Attachment Quotient (AQ) to refer to the capacity to connect to others in an emotionally meaningful way. The Attachment Quotient (AQ) is a person's sum bandwidth to connect with another. Our AQ is the result of an accumulation of many life experiences and also has a biological component; some of us are "wired" to connect more than others. Our AQ is largely formed in the early years based on the quality of the attachments we have with our mother and other important early figures in our life. Poor attachment to early caregivers, negligence, or trauma might result in a low AQ, whereas the presence of attentive, consistent, loving others who have the ability to understand our emotions might contribute to a high AQ.

You know when you sit down with someone whether they have a high AQ by the feeling that is generated as you sit with this person. Do you feel alone and disconnected, or do you feel welcomed and ready to share and connect? Does your body feel at ease, is there a relaxed smile on your face, or are you constricted, scanning for something you are not getting or feeling alone?

While generally a stable aspect of your character, your AQ can be situationally compromised if you're distracted or engaged in the more hyper-rational thinking that usually overrides the capacity to connect emotionally. "I'm trying to send an email, and my child is asking for an empathic response to a problem." The emotion is buried in the focused activity. In a culture like ours that values the hyper-rational and where executive functioning—planning, organizing, staying focused—is highly rewarded, emotional connection becomes collectively diluted. When our mind is engaged in efficiency, competition, and the type of mental activity oriented toward outcome, emotions of bonding are largely unavailable. The adult patients I see who are particularly successful in their careers, high-powered entrepreneurs or CEOs among others, are often afflicted with the inability to turn off this efficiency grid and engage in the world of the heart.

When you as a parent are in this hyper-focused, non-heart-centered mode, frustration and anger at your teen may be triggered at the slightest provocation. The ability to tolerate the messiness of being human—your teen once again complaining about her friends or her hair—is seen as "inefficient." And while this is true, you know by your frustration and your teen's earnest desire for you to understand their emotional world that what is true is not always what is helpful or what will yield meaningful connection.

The stark reality is that you cannot attach and connect in this overly cognitive operational mode. You know when you go too far in this type of super-logical activity because you start to feel detached or disconnected from yourself. Or someone reacts in a way that demands an emotional response, and all you can do is argue that their feelings are irrational. If you're disconnected from yourself, how can you connect to your teen?

7

TRANSFORMATIVE STRATEGY #7:
GO WITHIN

How you engage with your teen's troubles can be medicine for your own soul. When you exhaust the external solutions for your teen's problems—change schools, more sports, less discipline, no phone, more time together, no more tattoos, don't yell, do yell!—you are left with turning inward as a map through your teen's challenging terrain. This chapter is about the riches to be found when you peel back all the layers of self. It is about the aspects of self that can emerge: a new career, hobby, attitude, relationship, spiritual belief system, and more, all of these in tandem with your teen's growth. Bringing forth what is within is an extension of finding your purpose; it requires the most complete examination of self, unconscious and conscious, known and unknown, and requires even more courage than finding purpose because it requires a particular type of surrender that is only for the bold and brave. This is you!

There's a reason this chapter comes at the end, as the seventh transformative strategy. This excavation relies heavily on a solid knowledge of our emotions, through the work that is done through the first six transformative strategies. Because our teens are indeed presenting real-world dilemmas like substance use, depression, STS (snotty teen syndrome), and other challenges, we are often justifiably distracted by these outer problems and thus are even less likely to turn inward. But as Jung wrote, "Our wholeness is tested mercilessly." I believe this applies mightily to time with your teen.

When you feel the pain, only then can bliss emerge. In essence, all emotions, good and bad, are stored in the same little box inside. This does not mean that there are not objective actions to be taken that relate to your teen's behaviors. Of course, you need to say and do certain things at certain times to guide, dissuade, and support them, to set limits and to react in all the appropriate ways as a parent. But the truth is that your own unresolved emotions will make doing any of that less successful because you will be reacting from a place of exaggeration or a place of your own particular story, which will just interfere with and ruin anything else you are trying to achieve. By this point in the book, I hope you know a little bit about those pain points, that narrative, how you typically think, feel, and react to the world around you. And how you habitually see your teen, regardless of what they say or do.

Some of my patients wish to access the pleasure and bypass the pain. Unfortunately, it doesn't work that way. It's *through* the pain that you clear, burn, and create the path for pleasure. Bringing forth from within means first knowing how to go within and why. When your teen is struggling, it seems the last thing on your list is to think about yourself. But therein lie the truest and most profound answers, no matter the pain that gets us there. In my experience, when parents turn inward to give birth to something new in themselves, even in the midst of their child's darkest hours, it sheds a particular light on their teen's issues and can be healing for all. So let's proceed to the process of finding these inner jewels.

TRANSFORMATION IN PRACTICE: JANE, IRIS, AND MOLLY

Jane and Iris's story of parenting their daughter, Molly, is an example of how an authentic and deep sense of passion in parents' lives can unlock their teen's healing and power.

Jane and Iris adopted Molly at birth, and they came to me when Molly was seventeen and suffering from an eating disorder. What unfolded in the work with Jane and Iris was that each had deep conflicts about their own body images that they hid through politically articulated (but not emotionally felt) "pro-body" messages. In other words, they knew it was "right" to love their bodies as women, but they did not actually feel this aspect of self-love from the inside out. "Your body is beautiful exactly how it is," they would reassure Molly, who had started to care more about being thin than either mother thought was healthy. And they were right. But their encouragement was not supported by their own acceptance of their bodies.

The summer programs meant to support Molly's self-esteem did not translate to Molly's psyche, which continued to be affected by her parents' unresolved relationships to weight, self-image, and pleasing others versus finding their own authentic voices. Jane and Iris were largely well-adjusted women. Like many parents, their particular issues (in this case related to eating and body image) had never emerged until they had a daughter who was facing them. It is common that parents have a "good enough" grip on some of their issues until their child is suffering and pushes them to a new level of growth and self-understanding.

As we unraveled each of their dilemmas around body and self-image, it became clear that not only had Jane and Iris overshadowed Molly with their strongly held beliefs, leaving her no room for any normal bad feelings about herself (we all have good and bad feelings), but that they had devoted their lives to their daughter to the point of burying some important aspects of themselves. And while all parents do this to some extent, there are times when to do so is more disruptive than helpful. If you are suppressing a strong part of yourself, eventually it will manifest in some way, either in an illness or in a dysfunction in another part of your life—or in this case, in your child.

As Molly began to explore her feelings more authentically, and her moms also revealed previously unconscious and unresolved anxieties about their own bodies, Molly and her parents began to clear space for a more real and passionate connection to themselves and to their own previously unlived lives. Iris had left the field of graphic design to work in sales, which she described as "soul-killing," after adopting Molly. As the truths about their deeper emotions were revealed, Iris decided to take a chance and enroll in some art courses to see if she could integrate her lifelong passion for design into her life. This shifted her sense of self and her sense of body, which paralleled Molly's slow recovery and ultimate acceptance of her own body.

You may say it's a luxury to have the time and economic means to ponder one's passions. Yet the truth is that in my work with clients from all points on the economic spectrum, I have found that passion can be found in driving a sanitation truck or being a gardener as easily as it can in painting a canvas or running an investment firm. It's what's inside and how connected we are to ourselves that matters. And of course, every moment of our day cannot be a revelation as we deal with the realities of earning money, supporting ourselves, and raising a family. But in my experience shepherding hundreds of parents of varying economic means in and out of jobs, there are definitely some who are finding a deeper, more joyful experience in their day-to-day lives without giving up the hard responsibilities of life. Indeed, we need a modicum of material comfort to entertain this opportunity. But we can make a choice to engage in work that brings misery and shallowness or dive into life and "take a bite out of it," as it were, no matter what the task. In *A General Theory of Love*, Thomas Lewis, Fari Amini, and Richard Lannon describe this slow process of being seen and then finding that deeper connection to self:

> Those who succeed in revealing themselves to another find the dimness receding from their own visions of self. Like people awakening from a dream, they slough off the accumulated, ill-fitting trappings of unsuitable lives. Then the mutual fund manager may become a sculptor, or vice versa; some friendships lapse into dilapidated irrelevance as new ones deepen; the city dweller moves to the country, where he feels finally at home. As limbic clarity emerges, a life takes form.*

EXERCISE: BECOMING FEARLESS

Going within requires a certain fearlessness that we often do not embrace until we're desperate. You may realize you are not having the desired effect on your teen's challenges. Or perhaps your teen is really in trouble in some way. Or maybe she has triggered you to what you feel is a point of no return. Here's an exercise that will facilitate revealing the gem within even as you may be feeling the opposite: despair, frustration, or just plain exhaustion at the situation with your adolescent.

For each of the next ten days, do something you are afraid of, or contemplate a fear. First write a list of your fears, starting with mild ones and then recording more intense ones.

---

*Thomas Lewis, Fari Amini, and Richard Lannon, *A General Theory of Love* (New York: Vintage Books, 2000), 170.

A mild fear might be admitting how dependent you are on your child, and a more severe fear might be fear of facing your own inadequacy as a parent, or imagining your teen leaving the nest one day. Other fears might involve aspects of your work, losing your job, or other relationships. They may or may not relate to your teen but will be more relevant to your parenting if they do. Most fears are grounded in the same places within us, so the manifestation or the fear you choose to face is less important than the act of facing that fear and moving past it. The way you face your fears might be through an action: allowing your teen more freedom. Or it could be through a meditative act: contemplating and becoming more aware of your perceived inadequacies so as to accept them.

Start with something that elicits mild discomfort, and then increase the level of fear each day. Build your muscle of fearlessness.

TEEN TIP 101: EMPATHY INVITES THE DEEP GIFT OF CONNECTION

As you face fears and clear them, you leave room for the essential building blocks of parenting, such as empathy—the ability to walk in another's shoes. These nourishing capacities invite the connection that yields the gifts from within. When you are being held hostage by your past, it is nearly impossible to remain steady as your teen pushes and pulls you through their adventures. Getting to your authentic self is not possible without empathy for your teen; otherwise you are engaged in the blame game, and your focus is on how they are doing something wrong. The well-intended parents I work with, like all of us, have blind spots where they feel the most discomfort. Having empathy can be very challenging when you are up against these places in yourself. Empathy is not only important for your own growth but also the most effective way to reach your teen.

Teenagers are more likely to hear you when you are able to tell them how you feel rather than criticize them.* The exercises and meditations in this book are all tools to achieve the difficult but ultimately rewarding goal of knowing how you feel amid the myriad distractions and triggers your teen will elicit. It's simple but not easy. This is why I offer numerous exercises, as I have found that variety and practice support the deepest and most sustained results.

TRANSFORMATION IN PRACTICE: SALLY AND ZOE

Alicia, a single mom who worked for a technology company as a programmer, came into the first session reporting that "emotions are a bit foreign to me." This challenge was mirrored in her daughter, Zoe, age seventeen, who was so unskilled at handling emotions and so starved for someone to understand that she was cutting herself, superficially, to numb the emotional pain of loneliness. Zoe's schoolwork was overwhelming her, and the rest was a jumble. "I'm just very sad, and for no reason it seems. I have all these nice

---

*Adele Faber and Elaine Mazlish, *How to Talk So Teens Will Listen and Listen So Teens Will Talk* (New York: HarperCollins, 2005), 143.

things around me. I should be happy. I'm a defect," she would report each session.

When parents are unable to hold, understand, and make sense of their children's feelings, children and teens alike get the message that their feelings are superfluous. Often they even think they are bad for *having* feelings. Remember, humans have a deep evolutionary imperative embedded in many of their feelings and behaviors. Children, in particular, because of their profound dependency on parents, orient many of their emotional conclusions around what is good for their parents. For a child, the survival of their parents is their number one concern. So if parents are unable to understand or are otherwise dismissive of their child's emotions, the message to the child goes something like, "Bad kid. Cut that out, whatever it is. It's not having a good response from the person responsible for your survival." This message affects the child's development in a number of ways. Not only will he not be able to recognize and understand his own emotions but he will likely struggle to empathize with others. Additionally, as emotions form the foundation of our essential sense of self—what is truly inside us rather than the messages we receive about how to behave from society—finding a true experience in relationships or work can be compromised by these early failures to know our emotions through our parents' mirroring and understanding of them.

Our parents teach us about our emotions by responding to them with empathy and by unpacking them for us. (Or not!) Unfortunately, as loving and devoted as Alicia was to her daughter, this capacity was not in her repertoire. Zoe would plead through tears, "I just want someone who can give me a hug and let me cry. My mom tries—she puts pillows around me and brings me the snacks I like. I know she cares. But she just doesn't get it, and she gets so nervous when I am upset."

In my work with Mom and Zoe, we uncovered deep emotional rivers in both that hadn't been traversed in years, if ever. As we delved into grief, lost hopes, and vulnerabilities, Alicia became more able to relate to her daughter's feelings, most of which were completely normal. It was only because they had no outlet that they were perverted into depression. This process was immensely healing for Zoe. She stopped considering suicide as a means to solve what felt like unbearable pain and was able to receive comfort from her mom, who now had access to her own wider range of emotions.

EXERCISE: MOVING TOWARD THE GIFT

Using our reactions to our teen as an indicator of our own resistance is one way of looking within and moving toward our most authentic self. There are also other ways to become aware of the pain that holds the pleasure. Here are some questions you can ask yourself to begin to penetrate to the deeper waters and retrieve the pearl.

- What are you resisting in your own life? If you feel comfortable, ask your spouse, a sibling, a trusted friend. Take a few friends to coffee and spend twenty-five minutes as a group giving feedback to each other on the topic "What am I resisting?" Our friends can often see our blocks (behaviors, emotions, attitudes) and our gifts more clearly than we can. Note: take a deep breath and invite your least-defended self to show up and hear what it needs to hear.

- What emotion or experience do you consistently avoid? For some it is loneliness, for others shame or the experience of intimacy or vulnerability. For others, it is connecting to their children because it stirs up so much unresolved sadness related to disconnection from their own parents that they are avoiding their emotions and their children. If you find yourself feeling that your teen just "isn't enough" and there is a constant stream of criticism about them running through your mind, consider that this is your own experience of shame, of not being "good enough" being projected onto your teen. This particular "not enough" feeling can be expressed in obvious or subtle ways.

- Are you using substances to mute or manage feelings? Don't ask your teens to resist alcohol and other substances and expect them to listen if you are not willing to do so or at least have the capacity to do so yourself. Makes sense, right? We don't need to be perfect, just *aware* of how all our thoughts and behaviors influence those around us. We all have vices and suboptimal ways of handling life. Some of us cry; some get mad; some drink or use technology. The parents who seem to successfully stay connected to their teens aren't perfect, but they are self-aware enough that they know when they are engaging in numbing out or avoiding emotions or aspects of life. Your teen appreciates your awareness, your apologies, and your efforts at trying to be better. That's all you can offer.

- If you stop moving for a moment, what's the first feeling that comes up? Often we have habitual feeling states that are the "go-to" emotions for us. Sometimes they are the core feelings; sometimes they are the secondary emotions. For example, anger is usually a secondary emotion that is covering sadness. Irritation at being interrupted by your teen when you're writing an email that can wait may be hiding an ambivalence about connecting. Or the rage that erupts at this interruption could have a deeper root in a feeling of "not good enough" as you struggle to finish the last item on that to-do list. (Have you noticed that the list is never complete? Is your sense of "completeness" reliant on getting that last item done?) On your deathbed what will matter? Having completed the to-do list or having created space inside yourself to be present with your child? These questions are important because you can become convinced that the people around you—your teen, for example—are "doing things" to make you angry, sad, or disappointed. Sometimes—often, in fact—this is true. However, if we are inclined to experience these as baseline emotions, or if they are lingering just below the surface, undoubtedly our teen will pull at them and bring them out. It's just the way it seems to work.

- Complete the sentence, "My teen is so _____."
  Fill in with an emotion. Now ask yourself: Is this you
  or your teen? Many people who have a style of deep
  avoidance of feelings express them somatically—that is,
  in their body. Do you have consistent and chronic pain
  anywhere in your body that might provide a clue to
  where you hold emotion? Stomachaches? Headaches?
  A stuckness in your throat? A powerful form of therapy, Somatic Experiencing, invites us to delve into the
  language of the body to uncover trauma and even less
  severe emotions to heal them. Other types of therapies
  and energetic healing share this goal.

DON'T FEAR WHAT'S WITHIN

In my work with hundreds of intelligent and well-meaning
parents, I am struck by the power of their untold stories to
generate pain in relation to their children. "I know my mom
was severely depressed and never there for me in any way,"
one mother recounted. "But I'm over it. I don't want to go
there. How is drowning in my own darkness going to help
shed light on my son's depression?" she would ask when I
invited her to look inside.

Or more subtle but often equally painful insults from
childhood ("I was never listened to") can come out in needing
to lecture and control their children to the point of driving
them away. Parents whose pain has been severe often tout the
rewards of self-sufficiency as an answer. "I know my son has
it inside himself to figure this out," one dad insisted. And of

course this is partially true: we must find the strength from inside. Yet while self-sufficiency is an aspect of a healthy adult, I find that parents who have not healed their own wounds often wish their teens to be, like them, more self-sufficient than is actually healthy. "We are all pull-yourself-up-by-your-own-bootstraps kind of people," this dad remarked proudly. He attributed the multigenerational focus on independence as a hallmark of his family's success, and he lamented his teenage son's interest in staying at home to attend a community college as evidence of some sort of weakness.

But as the authors of *A General Theory of Love* note, "Total self-sufficiency turns out to be a daydream whose bubble is burst by the sharp edge of the limbic brain. Stability means finding people who regulate you well and staying near them."[*] Alienating your teen, a source of potential connection and limbic regulation, should not be done lightly. But it can happen if you cannot find the space to relate to yourself.

EMBODYING HOME

To embody home is one of the most rewarding and challenging roles you can hold as a parent. Before you find the deeper rewards in yourself, or expect your teen to find their passions, you both need a stable place from which to grow. If you are wobbly from your own inner challenges and distress, how do you provide that place to which your teen can return? Because you are inextricably linked to your child, as a parent you may

---

[*]Lewis, Amini, and Lannon, *A General Theory of Love.*

feel you can only move on to your own self-healing after you know your teen is okay. The "put your own oxygen mask on first" approach can almost feel selfish. I get it—I'm a mom. But what I see in my practice is parents who forget to fasten their own oxygen mask even *after* attending to their child's.

Studies show that the best outcome for successful maturation of adolescents happens in the relationship to their parents. So healing yourself as a parent is intertwined with caring for your teen. In order for your teen—so interested in all that is not you—to wish to maintain an attachment to you, you need to be a role model who is ever-evolving, just the way you wish your child to be. If you are frozen in your tracks, unable to see beyond your own neuroses, what can you expect from your teen? If you are only focused on them, how are you providing an example of how humans care for themselves while also having empathy and service for others? By acknowledging that you are a work in progress, you give your teen the permission to be messy, imperfect, and in transformation also.

TRANSFORMATION IN PRACTICE: BILL AND SEBASTIEN

The story of Bill and Sebastien illustrates the deep rewards that can be found when we go within. Bill, a successful lawyer who built his reputation on being right and righteous, struggled with his son's lack of truth telling. I call it "lack of truth telling" not to soften the problematic aspect of lying but to bring parents out of the moral zone, which is an important one but sometimes not the first place to start in addressing issues with teens. Teens elude the truth for many reasons. In this case, Sebastien, age eighteen, was doing it to gain some independence.

His parents were still treating Sebastien, now technically an adult, more like a fifteen-year-old: they were monitoring his activities and constantly giving him their advice on everything from dating to job finding. His "lies" posed no harm to him or to his parents. And when caught, he would apologize and acknowledge it as wrong. Still, his father's response was to go nuclear when he found out Sebastian had not told the truth. Bill had had a rigid upbringing with an authoritative father who was "always right," which did not allow for nuanced emotional realities.

After a few sessions in which I worked with him to help him learn the best way to stay connected to his son—which in fact would be the only way to ultimately impart his strong moral lessons—Bill was able to be more flexible. He was able to see his own rigid behavior by reflecting on the difficult personalities of his siblings. It's usually easier for us to see our faults in others before we see them in ourselves. Bill recounted stories about his sister's failed relationships, trips to rehab for substance use, and emotional outbursts that alienated family members. We gently moved to his own behavior, and because the pain with his son was so acute, he was able to take a look at his own black-and-white approach to his life and to his son. This awareness gave him more patience when talking to Sebastien. Consequently, Sebastien didn't feel the need to lie as he felt more understood and appreciated. This process, resulting in Bill's capacity to inhabit the gray zone in life rather than bouncing back and forth from black to white, indeed "saved" Bill and Sebastien's relationship and mined the riches that deep relationships can yield.

EXERCISE: VISUALIZATION TO IDENTIFY WHERE EMOTIONS LIVE IN OUR BODIES

Let's mine the riches of the body to see what we can bring forth that is being held in the nonverbal realm. If this might sound a bit "out there" for you, try this exercise anyway. I have found that even the most skeptical clients who have been willing to give these exercises a try usually emerge with something of value.[*]

Close your eyes. Breathe deeply into your belly. Surround yourself with gold, as if you are sitting in a golden orb. Then, send a grounding cord, made of any substance you like, to ground you to a place that feels safe. It can be the center of the Earth, or it can be a star. It can be anywhere that helps you feel centered as you sit in the gold orb, anywhere that helps you establish a sense of safety, calm, and contact with a more loving vibration, whatever that means to you. Next, start at your feet and scan your body for tightness, flutters, pain. Ask your body, "Where am I holding aspects of being not at ease?" "Where am I holding disharmony?" Go to that place. *Feel* into it. Palpate it—bring your awareness there.

Now: What does it *feel like*? What is it made of? Is it hard, soft, viscous, moving, still? What color is it? Now ask that

---

[*]I learned this exercise in a workshop led by Chris Griscom in Galisteo, New Mexico, in 2001.

place what color or colors does it need to be to come into perfect balance and harmony? Draw that color in from the top of your head into that place of dis-ease. Fill it up with that color. Take your time. Open your eyes.

Questions from the Body Scan

- Where were you holding the pain or discomfort?
- If you recontact that place, what emotion best describes the feeling you identified as painful? Is this a familiar feeling?
- How does your relationship to your teen get entangled with this feeling or set of feelings? Can you extract your teen from this place that is essentially inside of you?

Hot Seat Questions: Letting the Discomfort Speak to Bring Forth Truth

Now that you have listened exquisitely to your body's emotional messages, you can use this information to inquire about your everyday life with your teen and other family members. Those are the people who help us grow because they cut to the bone in our interactions with them.

- Is there any feedback that you get from your teen or partner that you consistently deny but that *could* have a grain of truth?
- What are you avoiding in yourself? What gift or skill or energetic contribution are you not sharing with the world because you are too busy thinking about or "do-

ing" for your teen beyond the point where they need you? Are you the micromanager? Or are you constantly singing and dancing across the kitchen? Are you always showing your friends and family iPhone photos of your kids? Are you the mom in the neighborhood who always has some remedy that you've concocted for ailing teens? Is your home the social center, and do you thrive on this type of energy?

- How do you manage anxiety? Do you need more support than you are getting?
- What is your life purpose? Your soul journey? Are you engaged in it every day?

EIGHT STEPS TO IDENTIFYING YOUR PASSION

Now is the time to go within!

1. Identify your passion. You know you're in your passion when you feel fearless. Getting in touch with your passion is also your economic advantage. People who are driven by their passion wake up earlier, work harder, and are less distracted by activities that would move them away from their goals. Intention plus right action produces amazing, speedy results. Find time every day to connect to your passion. You might connect to it through exercise, writing, painting, listening to music, even doing dishes. As one mom commented, "I'm on my own, and I'm doing dishes. It's a Zen moment."

2. Overcome emotional blocks. Fear is part of being human. Successful people get things done despite their fears. They know what kinds of structures they need, and they put them in place. Mourn the loss of who you think you need to be, and embrace who you are. As Freud said, "Out of your vulnerability will come your strength." Don't be afraid to feel your way to your passion.

3. Identify the skills you have developed as a parent. Multitasking, managing a household, and social-emotional fluency (reading a situation at a glance and knowing exactly what to do, like when you break up a fight between kids at the park) are transferable skills. Talk them up.

4. Use the Law of Attraction. Positive thoughts are paramount, especially in times of doom and gloom, because they attract positive experiences. Write down a sampling of your thoughts three times a day to make sure they're positive.

5. Dispel the myth of having it all. There is no utopian balance to achieve. Every choice has a sacrifice. Get comfortable with uncomfortable feelings, like guilt for not being home for dinner, fear of not doing it right, discomfort of being judged for a messy home.

6. Identify objectives clearly so the universe can deliver. Crystal clear goals get results. Vague hopes don't. If you have four hours a week to devote to yourself while your teen is in school, don't expect to do all your errands, exercise, *and* look for a job. Establish your priorities, and know how you will use your time, or it will disappear.

7. Take a step into the unknown. And trust that an opening will occur. "I want to know that it will lead somewhere that makes it worth taking away time from my teen." That's a sentiment all busy parents can relate to. But the truth is that you can't know the end before you begin. The universe rewards each step, even though you might not know what's next.

8. Live on the edge. If you're not living on the edge, you're taking up too much room.

BRINGING IT ALL TOGETHER

Teens, it turns out, are their parents' greatest teachers. Through your teen's intense and seemingly unendurable challenges, you find aspects of yourself that have been lost along the way and develop capacities that you've never had. By shifting how you experience your teen and using these principles, both you and your teen can grow in these otherwise irritating and sometimes even dangerous times. What you fear becomes what you face; your greatest weakness becomes your saving strength. In the very situations that bring you to the darkest edge, that seem to offer no way out, a patient application of certain processes brings more wisdom and joy. Through a sometimes circuitous path, both you and your teen find aspects of yourselves that could not have been discovered if not for this particular type of travel together.

Staying connected with yourself and your teen and slowing down are key features of reaping these benefits. Surrendering to the reality of what your teen brings rather than clinging to your illusions of what you believe should be is another helpful activity. Looking at your deepest resistance, you find the greatest openings for possibilities. And accepting what you at first deemed as unacceptable in your teen and in yourself yields unknown opportunities that your mind could not have predicted or planned.

Why not grow as a person in this challenging time and use the troubles and joys your teen presents as opportunities for your own expansion? The unresolved dilemmas within you as a parent may never be granted the opportunity for resolution if not for your obnoxious and sometimes terrifying teenager! Giving birth to this adult child takes a particular type of courage that some come by naturally and others need to cultivate and practice. Of course, sometimes your teen's behaviors and attitudes are uniquely their own; no matter what you do, they will continue on with their own journey untouched by whatever you do, say, or become. But I have found that this is the rare case.

Endure emotions. Enlarge the lens. Don't grasp—let go. Discover profound purpose. Contemplate infinite possibility. Heal thyself. Go within. All of these transformative strategies may sound simple, but none of them is easy.

As we reach the close of this book, I invite you to ask yourself what you have learned so far about yourself with your teen. What are you most surprised about that has been brought forth, perhaps from a deep place, to heal you and have a positive impact on your adolescent? This realization could be emotional, spiritual, or vocational. It could be something you don't like to do or a characteristic that you know you are not interested in developing. Or it could be an interest that has emerged through plumbing the depths of your emotions, or through meditating, or even through being triggered.

What pain have you had to endure? Okay, there's more than one, I'm sure. Can you withdraw the projection and blame? Are you able to take the sentence, "My teen is so . . . that it makes me feel . . . " and rewrite that sentence to honor the experiences that are *yours*? Is there gratitude for having them? Can you find the noble side of fear? The sweet aspects of loss? The beauty in betrayal? How are you with practicing paradox?

What data points on your personal map have you discovered so far through the relationship with your teen? Data points are like stars in your personal sky or authentic emotional moments that you never would have discovered, such as a new hobby or a love of dogs. It could be anything. It could come from triggers or the relationship with your teen.

One woman I worked with discovered that she was a master organizer after unhooking from micromanaging her son's life. Another realized the plains of Africa were to be her new point of exploration after forcing her daughter to go hiking in the hills near their house every day. It was *Mom* who truly wanted that experience of merging with nature and losing herself in the wildlife surrounding her home. A father discovered his tenderness through working through his sky-high expectations of his son. By working through the disappointment that his son dragged him through (failing out of high school, a marijuana addiction, both of which resolved), Dad was able to discover the joy of vulnerability and loosen his own impossibly high expectations of himself.

Where are you still in the dark? That is, what part of your teen can you still not accept? Which part of *yourself* can you still not accept? Where's the expansion into the truth of your teen that you need to allow? And similarly, where do you still have room to grow?

EPILOGUE

T HE TEEN'S STRUGGLE: I DON'T KNOW WHO I AM, BUT don't try to tell me. And don't criticize me or try to give me too much advice, especially when I really mess up. Because my job is to figure it out all by myself. The birth of the new self has not yet been complete. Parents are equally lost at times. They, too, are in a process of birthing a self as they ride this wave with their teen. Parents and their teens are all trying to find their way.

How do you practice your strengths and admit your weaknesses so that you can expand with your teen rather than remain frozen in your own unproductive patterns? I invite you to be courageous and use your heart—especially when it feels broken. (The word "courageous" comes from the French word for heart, *coeur*.) Practice the paradoxes that your teen will invite: come close, go away, I love you, I hate you. Find your own center as he pushes you to your edge.

The practices I have outlined aren't meant to be read once. This book is not linear but, like life and like healing, should be taken as a spiral. Revisit Chapter 2 after you complete Chapter 7. Underline passages; practice exercises again and again; highlight examples of parents and teens who resonate with your own hurts and joys.

If you engage in these practices and let them percolate and become familiar, I trust that you will find the expansive pause, the ability to entertain more options, and the capacity to generate more useful solutions to the power struggles. Reaction will yield to moments of spaciousness and considered response. You will notice your teen shifting, perhaps in small moments at first, but then in more consistent emotional and behavioral changes. They will find shelter in your self-awareness, peace in your steady gaze. No matter the influence of friends, culture, and everything their phone can offer, if you stay connected to your teen, you will always be a place of refuge and influence.

My hope is that through reading these pages, your desire to connect more intimately with yourself, through your teen's challenges, has been ignited. So the next time your teen flips you the bird, demands something ridiculous, gets drunk, or engages in any other of the many unlovable behaviors they have in their repertoire, you can pull from these exercises to move into your body, understand your own patterns of wounding, and go to Spirit—to find the love instead of the fear. When you see your teen as your teacher, you will have a humility and an openness to grace and opportunity that will yield infinite possibility. I hope that this book has opened a new vista for you and your teen. A place of connection and solace where the problems can be transformed into better and better solutions. For love.

FURTHER RESOURCES

Aron, Elaine. *The Highly Sensitive Person: How to Thrive When the World Overwhelms You.* New York: Broadway Books, 1996.

Bayard, Robert, and Jean Bayard. *How to Deal with Your Acting-Up Teenager: Practical Self-Help for Desperate Parents.* Lanham, MD: M. Evans & Company, 1981.

Beck, Martha. *Finding Your Way in a Wild New World: Reclaim Your True Nature to Create the Life You Want.* New York: Free Press, 2012.

Blos, Peter. *On Adolescence.* New York: Free Press of Glencoe, 1962.

Bollas, Christopher. *The Shadow of the Object: Psychoanalysis of the Unthought Known.* New York: Columbia University Press, 1987.

Bolton, Nick. "Steve Jobs Was a Low-Tech Parent." *New York Times,* September 10, 2014.

Bradshaw, John. *Homecoming: Reclaiming and Championing Your Inner Child.* New York: Bantam Books, 1992.

Chopra, Deepak. *The Seven Spiritual Laws of Success: A Practical Guide to the Fulfillment of Your Dreams.* San Rafael, CA: Amber-Allen Publishing and New World Library, 1994.

Faber, Adele, and Elaine Mazlish. *How to Talk So Teens Will Listen and Listen So Teens Will Talk.* New York: HarperCollins, 2005.

Friedman, Thomas. *Thank You for Being Late: An Optimist's Guide to Thriving in the Age of Acceleration.* New York: Farrar, Straus and Giroux, 2016.

Gerber, Richard. *Vibrational Medicine: The #1 Handbook of Subtle-Energy Therapies.* Rochester, VT: Bear & Co., 2001.

Griscom, Chris. *Ecstasy Is a New Frequency: Teachings of the Light Institute.* Santa Fe: Bear & Co., 1987.

Hari, Johann. "The Likely Cause of Addiction Has Been Discovered, and It Is Not What You Think." *Huffington Post,* January 20, 2015.

Hartley-Brewer, Elizabeth. *Talking to Tweens: Getting It Right Before It Gets Rocky with Our 8- to 12-Year-Old.* Cambridge, MA: Da Capo, 2005.

Iyengar, B. K. S. *Light on Yoga.* New York: Schocken Books, 1996.

Jung, C. G. *Selected Letters of C. G. Jung, 1909–1961.* Princeton, NJ: Princeton University Press, 1984.

Kohn, Alfie. *The Brighter Side of Human Nature: Altruism and Empathy in Everyday Life.* New York: Basic Books, 1990.

———. *Unconditional Parenting: Moving from Rewards and Punishments to Love and Reason.* New York: Atria Books, 2005.

Lamott, Anne. *Operating Instructions: A Journal of My Son's First Year.* New York: Anchor Books, 1993.

Levine, Madeline. *The Price of Privilege: How Parental Pressure and Material Advantage Are Creating a Generation of Disconnected and Unhappy Kids.* New York: HarperCollins, 2006.

Levine, Peter. *Waking the Tiger: Healing Trauma.* Berkeley: North Atlantic Books, 1997.

Levine, Peter, and Maggie Line. *Trauma Proofing Your Kids: A Parents' Guide for Instilling Confidence, Joy and Resilience.* Berkeley: North Atlantic Books, 2008.

Lewis, Thomas, Fari Amini, and Richard Lannon. *A General Theory of Love.* New York: Vintage Books, 2000.

Linehan, Marsha. *DBT Skills Training Manual*. 2nd ed. New York: Guilford, 2015.

Neufeld, Gordon, and Gabor Mate. *Hold Onto Your Kids: Why Parents Need to Matter More Than Peers*. New York: Ballantine Books, 2006.

O'Donohue, John. *Anam Cara: A Book of Celtic Wisdom*. New York: HarperCollins, 1997.

Ponton, Lynn. *The Romance of Risk: Why Teenagers Do the Things They Do*. New York: Basic Books, 1987.

Sachs, Brad E. *The Good Enough Teen: Raising Adolescents with Love and Acceptance (Despite How Impossible They Can Be)*. New York: Perrenial Currents, 2005.

Siegel, Daniel J. *Brainstorm: The Power and Purpose of the Teenage Brain*. New York: Tarcher/Penguin, 2013.

Siegel, Daniel J., and Mary Hartzell. *Parenting from the Inside Out: How a Deeper Self-Understanding Can Help You Raise Children Who Thrive*. New York: Tarcher/Penguin, 2003.

Simon, Michael. *The Approximate Parent: Discovering the Strategies That Work with Your Teenager*. Oakland, CA: Fine Optics, 2012.

Steinberg, Laurence, and Ann Levine. *You and Your Adolescent: A Parent's Guide for Ages 10–20*. New York: HarperPerennial, 1990.

Stiffelman, Susan. *Parenting with Presence: Practices for Raising Conscious, Confident, Caring Kids*. Novato, CA: New World Library, 2015.

Welwood, John. *Perfect Love, Imperfect Relationships: Healing the Wound of the Heart*. Boston: Shambhala Publications, 2006.

Winnicott, D. W. *Home Is Where We Start From: Essays by a Psychoanalyst*. New York: W. W. Norton, 1986.

ACKNOWLEDGMENTS

A book is indeed a tapestry of varied voices; the sum ever greater than its parts.

Thank you to my wonderful agent, Sharon Bowers, who believed in my manuscript and found the perfect home for it at Hachette Book Group, Seal Press. Dr. Michelle Perro, thank you for connecting me with Sharon and for parenting the parent during my early days as a mother. A deep debt of gratitude must go to Jean-Michele Gregory, whose creative vision and masterful organizational instincts honed my message. She managed to put the spiraling nature of psychic change in linear terms; thank you, JM! Thank you to Stephanie Knapp at Seal Press for understanding the power of parental and teen growth through relationship and for seeing the potential impact of this book. Stephanie, your keen editorial eye and devotion to the manuscript has been unwavering. Thank you to the entire team at Seal Press, including Sharon Kunz, Matthew Weston, and all the dedicated staff at Hachette. Nancy Levine, my friend, how can I thank you for your gift of connecting people, grasping project execution, and putting your heart and mind into this effort on my behalf? I offer my first editor, Andrea Alban, much gratitude for providing guidance and wisdom in the early days of development. Maureen O'Brien, you saw the gem in the dross. Renae Bechtold, thank you for keeping me laser focused so that I could complete this book before I was too old to enjoy its fruits.

This book would not be possible without the support of my mentors: Richard Lannon, for offering ever more meaningful truths to my narrative. Thank you, Dr. Lannon, for imparting the mysteries of human connection. Dr. Fari Amini taught me that our patients become part of us. Thank you to my mentors at Yale, including Braxton McKee. Lynn Ponton, thank you for our dinner conversations about teenagers and your pioneering work in the field of adolescence. Chris Griscom, your lessons in the realms of higher consciousness and opportunities to walk on hot coals in Galisteo, New Mexico, have deeply informed my work as a healer. And I would be remiss if I didn't thank Mrs. Leerburger, my high school English teacher at SHS, for teaching me how to write in the first place.

Gratitude to all the professionals who have supported this work: Martin Rossman, MD; Michael Finkelstein, MD; Tom Allon; Glen Elliott, MD, PhD; Rhonda Adessky, PhD;

Paula Bennett; Tom Monaco; Bryna Siegel, PhD; and Sam Judice, MD.

Thank you to my friends and family; you are the love.

And thank you, last but certainly not least, to my patients with whom I have suffered and loved and without whom this offering could not be made.

INDEX

Index

ABOUT THE AUTHOR

Christa M. Santangelo, PhD, is a clinical psychologist specializing in the healing power of human relationship. Since completing her postdoctoral fellowship at Yale University, Dr. Santangelo has served as assistant clinical professor at the University of California at San Francisco (UCSF) and seen patients in her private practice in Marin County, California. Dr. Santangelo has twenty-five years of experience healing children, teens, and adults in medical settings and clinics and has received recognition for excellence in her teaching of psychiatry fellows at UCSF School of Medicine and UCSF Department of Psychiatry. She has also taught yoga in her community. Dr. Santangelo believes that the deepest emotional challenges afford the greatest opportunities for transformation. To this end, she provides a multimodal approach to healing that integrates conventional psychology with alternative medicine, including meditation and energy work. Dr. Santangelo is also a mother of a spirited daughter whom she parents with her devoted husband. She cherishes the bonds of connection—friends and family—with whom cooking and laughing provide deep nourishment and the true sustenance of her life. Dr. Santangelo believes that children, especially teens, have a particular wisdom that they must bring forth to evolve our species to a higher level of consciousness. For more about Dr. Santangelo, please visit www.christasantangelo.com.